跨文化交流英语技能训练与读本分析

黄　莉◎著

燕山大学出版社
·秦皇岛·

图书在版编目（CIP）数据

跨文化交流英语技能训练与读本分析 / 黄莉著．—秦皇岛：燕山大学出版社，2023.7
ISBN 978-7-5761-0499-8

Ⅰ．①跨… Ⅱ．①黄… Ⅲ．①英语－教学研究－高等学校 Ⅳ．①H319.3

中国国家版本馆 CIP 数据核字（2023）第 043887 号

跨文化交流英语技能训练与读本分析
KUAWENHUA JIAOLIU YINGYU JINENG XUNLIAN YU DUBEN FENXI
黄　莉　著

出 版 人： 陈　玉
责任编辑： 王　宁　　**策划编辑：** 王　宁
责任印制： 吴　波　　**封面设计：** 刘韦希
出版发行： 燕山大学出版社 YANSHAN UNIVERSITY PRESS　　**电　　话：** 0335-8387555
地　　址： 河北省秦皇岛市河北大街西段 438 号　　**邮政编码：** 066004
印　　刷： 秦皇岛墨缘彩印有限公司　　**经　　销：** 全国新华书店

开　　本： 710 mm×1000 mm　1/16　　**印　　张：** 15.25
版　　次： 2023 年 7 月第 1 版　　**印　　次：** 2023 年 7 月第 1 次印刷
书　　号： ISBN 978-7-5761-0499-8　　**字　　数：** 234 千字
定　　价： 60.00 元

前　言

目前，我国社会和高校对英语教育的观念发生了巨大变化，对英语基础课程的教学学时、内容、手段和方法，教材的编写与使用等都提出了更高的要求。本书基于新的社会历史文化语境，对于应用型高校非英语专业本科生英语认知、促进学生个性的发展和潜能的发挥具有一定的指导意义。

本书既注重英语语言基础知识的系统复习，又强调听、说、读、写、译五种技能的综合训练；既可用作全国大学英语四、六级考试的参考资料，也可作为中西方文化交流的读物。本书具有如下特点：

（1）模块化的内容架构。每个单元主题均贴近学生的生活现实，其情景的设置与学生在学校、社会及未来的生活密切相关。每单元都包括听、说、读、写、译五大模块，每个模块重点练习 2 ～ 3 种语言功能。

（2）知识性、趣味性与文化性并重。在语料的选择方面，注重语言素材与中西方文化的结合，融知识性、趣味性与文化性于一体，题材广泛，体裁多样，语料真实，语言地道，形式活泼，图文并茂。在内容的设计上，力求语言知识、文化意识与批判性思维能力培养并重。

（3）英语考级水平的训练。本书融入英语考试技巧和题型的训练，提供听、说、读、写、译五大模块的训练题，有针对性地提高学生的应试水平。

本书前七个单元的结构如下：

（1）单元目标：通过 Learning Objectives、Learning Difficult Points、Outline、Vocabulary 和 Looking Ahead，让学生感知本单元的学习目标、大纲、重难点、重要词汇和主要学习内容等。

（2）Listening：每单元提供相关的听力技巧与策略指导，并通过相关对话与短文的训练，提高学生的听力能力。

（3）Speaking：提出与主题相关的问题供学生探讨，既有利于后续课文的学习，也有利于引导学生主动、交互学习。

（4）Conversation：提供与主题相关的对话，通过会话练习提高学生的口语交际能力。

（5）Reading：由 Text A 和 Text B 组成，课文均选自英语国家人文作品，内容地道，原汁原味，每篇课文后配有相应的阅读理解练习，以更好地掌握学生的阅读理解情况。

（6）Writing：应用文写作帮助学生了解各种体裁的应用文的格式及写作方法。

（7）New Words and phrases：罗列出与 Text A 和 Text B 相关的词汇和短语。

（8）Extended Exercises：补充完形填空、信息匹配阅读和段落翻译等与全国大学英语四、六级考试最新题型相关的练习。

本书具有一定实用性，不仅有助于培养学生听、说、读、写、译各方面的能力，而且有助于提高学生全国大学英语四、六级考试的应试能力。

本书的编写是在校领导和有关部门的大力支持下完成的，在此，对校领导和学校师生所给予的支持与帮助表示最诚挚的谢意！同时，也希望师生多提宝贵意见，以便对书中不足之处加以完善。

目　　录

Unit 1 Optimism and Life Choice 1
Unit 2 My First Job 31
Unit 3 Art and Tourism 56
Unit 4 Mysteries of the Universe 86
Unit 5 People Who Changed the Shape of Our World 116
Unit 6 Moral Values 147
Unit 7 Modern Technology 176
Unit 8 English Literature 207

Unit 1 Optimism and Life Choice

Learning Objectives

After completing this unit, you will be able to do the following:

◇ Practice for the skill: How to identify News Lead;
◇ Grasp the main idea and the structure of the texts;
◇ Master the key language points and grammatical structure in the text;
◇ Conduct a series of reading, speaking and writing activities related to the theme in the unit.

Learning Difficult Points

In this unit, you will learn some difficult points listed below.
Listening: How to identify News Lead.
Writing: Applied Writing

Outline

The Following are the main sections in this Unit.

1. Listening
2. Speaking
3. Reading: Text A & Text B
4. Writing
5. Extended Exercises

Vocabulary

Listed below are some words appearing in this unit that you should make part of your vocabulary.

poverty
board
expired
extol
career
phenomenon
thrive (in)
reflect on
round the corner
scuttle off

Looking Ahead

Optimism and Life Choice

We cannot survive without food, clothes and other things we can get. But a worthy life does not depend on how much we can get; rather it depends on how much we can give others. Giving rather than taking, makes us different from other animals.

— Winston Churchill

Introduction

Mohandas Karamchand Gandhi believed that the way people behave is more important than what they accomplish. Gandhi studied law but became known for social action. He practiced non-violence to help India achieve independence from Britain.

Albert Schweitzer was born in Alsace, Germany, which is now a part of France. Before he was 30, he was a respected writer, an organist, and an expert on the life and work of John Sebastian Bach. In 1904, inspired to help sick people in the world, Schweitzer began to study medicine. Over the years, he built a large hospital that served thousands of Africans. In 1952, Schweitzer received the Nobel Prize for Peace.

Gandhi and Schweitzer had plans for their lives, but their plans changed. They made a real difference in their life.

Speaking

Consider the following questions before reading:

1. What were you going to do or be when you are young?
2. Did you change your mind? Talk about changes in your life plans.

Conversation

Role-play meeting someone you haven't seen for a while. Talk about changes in your life plans.

A: Hey, Robbie! Long time no see.

B: Richard! How have you been?

A: Not bad, thanks. So what are you doing these days?

B: Well, I'm in a dental school.

A: No Kidding! I thought you had other plans.

B: That's right. I was going to be an artist, but I changed my mind.

A: How come?

B: Well, I find my affection in teaching and I love kids.

A: Doing something good for others is good for you. Really.

UNIT 1 Optimism and Life Choice

Listening

Listening skills are fundamental to success in Listening. Through this part, we will have a detailed introduction to promote listening efficiency we could enhance by analyzing the three parts—News, Long conversation and Passage.

Listening Skills for News (1)

The technology, economy, social life, political organization, religions, art, involving culture and life affairs may be the variable contents of the News, which is reflected as students' most feared and uncontrollable parts in Listening Comprehension. The reasons for this phenomenon are as follows: few listening exercises at ordinary times, poor voice sensitivity and weak listening skills.

News reports are involved in a wide range of contents, but the language structure has a certain rule to follow. The first sentence of every news referred to as News Lead is the essential content of the news. Theoretically, News Lead should answer 5 questions of Ws and a H: What? Who? When? Where? Why and How? Though in actual reports, News Lead (introductions) generally answer only a few of the above 6 questions, it is still the theme of the news.

Keys to identify News Lead correctly :

Example（出自四级听力原文）

Big fast-food chains in New York City have started to obey a first-of-its-kind rule requiring them to post calorie counts right on the menu.

纽约市的大型快餐连锁店迎来了一项史无前例的新规定，这一规定要求他们在菜单上附上卡路里含量表。

Cathy Nonas is with the New York City Department of Health.

纽约市健康部的凯西·诺娜说：

"We wanted to give people an opportunity to actually see the calories before they purchase the food and make a decision, an informed decision,

"我们希望让消费者能够在知情的情况下作出购物决定。

that if they want to make the healthier choice, if they want to eat fewer calories, they can.

如果他们希望吃到更健康的食物，想摄入更少的热量，这是可以实现的。

And of course, if it has an impact on obesity, it will have an impact on diabetes, and heartdisease, and high blood pressure."

当然，如果它能改善肥胖问题，那么它也就会降低糖尿病、心脏病和高血压的患病率。"

The new rules were introduced as part of an anti-obesity campaign that also includes a recent citywide ban on artificial trans-fats in restaurant

导语（News Lead）回答了 What 和 Who 的问题，简明扼要地综述了新闻事件的要点。第 3 题可在导语中找到答案。

新闻主体（Body），它分析了制定新规定的原因 Why，以及如何实施新规定 How。新闻主体部分细节出分析题较多。

food.

这项规定是该城市最近发起的反肥胖症运动的一部分。此次反肥胖症运动还颁布了一条禁止全城餐馆使用人工反式脂肪的禁令。

The menu rule only applies to restaurants that serve standardized portion sizes and have 15 or more locations nationwide.

菜单新规只适用于提供标准化饮食分量、并在全国有 15 家或以上连锁店的餐馆。

Starting last Saturday, chains big enough to fall under the rule will face penalties of up to 2000 dollars for not showing calorie information in a prominent spot on their menus, preferably next to the price.

从上周六开始，符合条件的餐馆需要在其菜单明显位置，最好在价格旁边显示卡路里信息，否则将会面临多达 2000 美元的罚款。

Questions 3 and 4 are based on the news report you have just heard.

请根据你刚才听到的新闻报道回答问题 3 和问题 4。

3. What are big fast-food chains in New York City required to do according to the new rule?

新规定要求纽约市的大型快餐连锁店做什么？

4. What will happen to big restaurant chains that violate the new rule?

如果大型快餐连锁店违反规定将会怎样？

在这篇新闻中，“Big fast-food chains in New

第 4 题可在新闻结语中找到答案。呼应导语，纽约市的大型快餐连锁店如不遵守新规，将会面临多达 2000 美元的罚款。

York City have started to obey a first-of-its-kind rule requiring them to post calorie counts right on the menu.”就是导语，我们在收听新闻时，首先要听懂新闻导语，为下文的理解打下基础。

Reading

Text A

Warming-up Activity:

Joanne Rowling, (/ˈroʊlɪŋ/; born on 31 July 1965), who writes under the pen names J. K. Rowling and Robert Galbraith, is a British novelist and screenwriter who is best known for writing the Harry Potter fantasy series. The books have won multiple awards, and sold more than 400 million copies. They have become one of the best-selling book series in history and been the basis for a series of films, over which Rowling had overall approval on the scripts and was a producer on the final films in the series.

J. K. Rowling's commencement speech at Harvard University

President Faust, members of the Harvard Corporation and the Board of Overseers, members of the faculty, proud parents, and, above all, graduates.

The first thing I would like to say is "thank you". Not only has Harvard given me an extraordinary honor, but the weeks of fear and nausea I've endured at the thought of giving this commencement address have made me lose weight. A win-win situation! Now all I have to do is to take deep breaths, squint at the red banners and convince myself that I am at the world's largest Gryffindors' reunion.

Delivering a commencement address is a great responsibility; or so I thought until I cast my mind back to my own graduation. The commencement speaker that day was the distinguished British philosopher Baroness Mary Warnock. Reflecting on her speech has helped me enormously in writing this one, because it turns out that I can't remember a single word she said. This liberating discovery enables me to proceed without any fear that I might inadvertently influence you to abandon promising careers in business, law or politics for the giddy delights of becoming a gay wizard.

You see? If all you remember in years to come is the 'gay wizard' joke, I've still come out ahead of Baroness Mary Warnock. Achievable goals - the first step to self-improvement.

Actually, I have wracked my mind and heart for what I ought to say to you today. I have asked myself what I wish I had known at my own graduation, and what important lessons I have learned in the 21 years that has expired between that day and this.

I have come up with two answers. On this wonderful day when we are gathered together to celebrate your academic success, I have decided to talk to you about the benefits of failure. And as you stand on the threshold of what is sometimes called 'real life', I want to extol the crucial importance of imagination.

These may seem quixotic or paradoxical choices, but bear with me.

Looking back at the 21-year-old that I was at graduation, is a slightly uncomfortable experience for the 42-year-old that she has become. Half my lifetime ago, I was striking an uneasy balance between the ambition I had for myself, and what those closest to me expected of me.

I was convinced that the only thing I wanted to do, ever, was to write novels. However, my parents, both of whom came from impoverished backgrounds and neither of whom had been to college, took the view that my overactive imagination was an amusing personal quirk that could never pay a mortgage, or secure a pension.

I know the irony strikes like with the force of a cartoon anvil now, but...

They had hoped that I would take a vocational degree; I wanted to study English Literature. A compromise was reached that in retrospect satisfied nobody, and I went up to study Modern Languages. Hardly had my parents' car rounded the corner at the end of the road than I ditched German and scuttled off down the Classics corridor.

I cannot remember telling my parents that I was studying Classics; they might well have found out for the first time on graduation day. Of all the subjects on this planet, I think they would have been hard put to name one less useful than Greek mythology when it came to securing the keys to an executive bathroom.

I would like to make it clear, in parenthesis, that I do not blame my parents for their point of view. There is an expiry date on blaming your parents for steering you in the wrong direction; the moment you are old enough to take the wheel, responsibility lies with you. What is more, I cannot criticise my parents for hoping that I would never experience poverty. They had been poor themselves, and I have since been poor, and I quite agree with them that it is not an ennobling experience. Poverty entails fear, and stress, and sometimes depression; it means a thousand petty humiliations and hardships. Climbing out of poverty by your own efforts, that is indeed something on which to pride yourself, but poverty itself is romanticized only by fools.

What I feared most for myself at your age was not poverty, but failure.

At your age, in spite of a distinct lack of motivation at university, where I had spent far too long in the coffee bar writing stories, and far too little time at lectures, I had a knack for passing examinations, and that, for years, had been the measure of success in my life and that of my peers.

I am not dull enough to suppose that because you are young, gifted and well-educated, you have never known hardship or heartache. Talent and intelligence never yet inoculated anyone against the caprice of the Fates, and I do not for a moment suppose that everyone here has enjoyed an existence of unruffled privilege and contentment.

However, the fact that you are graduating from Harvard suggests that you are not very well-acquainted with failure. You might be driven by a fear of failure quite as much as a desire for success. Indeed, your conception of failure might not be too far from the average person's idea of success, so high have you already flown academically.

Ultimately, we all have to decide for ourselves what constitutes failure, but the world is quite eager to give you a set of criteria if you let it. So I think it fair to say that by any conventional measure, a mere seven years after my graduation day, I had failed on an epic scale. An exceptionally short-lived marriage had imploded, and I was jobless, a lone parent, and as poor as it is possible to be in modern Britain, without being homeless. The fears my parents had had for me, and that I had had for myself, had both come to pass, and by every usual standard, I was the biggest failure I knew.

Now, I am not going to stand here and tell you that failure is fun. That period of my life was a dark one, and I had no idea that there was going to be what the press has since represented as a kind of fairy tale resolution. I had no idea how far the tunnel extended, and for a long time, any light at the end of it was a hope rather than a reality.

So why do I talk about the benefits of failure? Simply because failure meant a stripping away of the inessential. I stopped pretending to myself that I was anything other than what I was, and began to direct all my energy into finishing the only work that mattered to me. Had I really succeeded at anything else, I might never have found the determination to succeed in the one arena I believed I truly belonged. I was set free, because my greatest fear had been realised, and I was still alive, and I still had a daughter whom I adored, and I had an old typewriter and a big idea. And so rock bottom became the solid foundation on which I rebuilt my life.

You might never fail on the scale I did, but some failure in life is inevitable. It is impossible to live without failing at something, unless you live so cautiously that you might as well not have lived at all-in which case, you fail by default.

Failure gave me an inner security that I had never attained by passing examinations. Failure taught me things about myself that I could have learned no other way. I discovered that I had a strong will, and more discipline than I had suspected; I also found out that I had friends whose value was truly above the price of rubies.

The knowledge that you have emerged wiser and stronger from setbacks means that you are, ever after, secure in your ability to survive. You will never truly know yourself, or the strength of your relationships, until both have been tested by adversity. Such knowledge is a true gift, for all that it is painfully won, and it has been worth more to me than any qualification I ever earned.

So given a Time Turner, I would tell my 21-year-old self that personal happiness lies in knowing that life is not a check-list of acquisition or achievement. Your qualifications, your CV, are not your life, though you will meet many people of my age and older who confuse the two. Life is difficult, and complicated, and beyond anyone's total control, and the humility to know that will enable you to survive its vicissitudes.

I wish you all very good lives.

Thank you very much.

Reading Exercises:

Directions: *In this section, you are required to complete each question by deciding on the most appropriate one from the 4 choices.*

1. The first thing J. K. Rowling would like to say is "thank you" for the reasons:

A. She graduated from Harvard University at the year 21.

B. Harvard gave her an extraordinary honor.

C. That she has endured at the thought of giving this commencement address has made her lose weight.

D. B and C

2. What does Rowling's Parents think of Rowling's career?

A. It is expected to take a vocational career.

B. It is not expected to take a vocational career.

C. It is expected to learn Classics .

D. It is expected to learn Modern Language.

3. What are we supposed to do towards failure?

A. We should try our best to avoid failures.

B. We should control our feeling and stay calm.

C. We should know the knowledge that you have emerged wiser and stronger from failure means that you are, ever after, secure in your ability to survive.

D. We should not let our sadness over losses prevent us from succeeding.

4. Which of the following statement is Not Correct?

A. What Rowling feared most for herself at young age was failure.

B. What Rowling feared most for herself at young age was poverty.

C. She cannot criticise her parents for hoping that she would never experience poverty.

D. She believes that is indeed something on which to pride yourself, but poverty itself is romanticized only by fools.

5. What does Rowling remind students as essentials to life?

A. Life is a check-list of acquisition or achievement

B. Qualifications.

C. CV.

D. Not mentioned.

New Words and Phrases

Text A:

poverty [ˈpɒvəti] *n.* state of being poor 贫穷；贫困

e.g. They refuse to do anything about the real cause of crime: poverty.

他们拒绝采取措施解决引发犯罪的真正问题：贫穷。

四级真题中的使用：

A stable family is the best protection against poverty.

determination [dɪˌtɜːmɪˈneɪʃn] *n.* quality of being firmly committed to doing sth. 决心（定）；坚决；果断

e.g. It is only our determination to fight that has pulled us through.

正是我们坚持战斗的决心帮我们渡过了难关。

四级真题中的使用：

his firm determination to win in the competition against his rivals

board [bɔːd] *n.* ① a group of people who have power to make decisions and control a company or other organization（公司或其他机构的）董事会，委员会，理事会 ② a long thin piece of strong hard material, especially wood, used, for example, for making floors, building walls and roofs and making boats 板；（尤指）木板

v. ① to get on a ship, train, plane, bus, etc. 上船（或火车、飞机、公共汽车等） ② to live and take meals in sb.'s home, in return for payment 付费（在某人家里）膳宿

e.g. The board is/are unhappy about falling sales.

董事会对销售额下降感到不满。

四级真题中的使用：

1. Universities like Cornell and Brown have jumped on board.
2. This has been due, in part, to the Bill and Melinda Gates Foundation, which has invested $1.8 billion in American high schools, helping to open about 1,000 small schools-most of them with about 400 kids each, with an average enrollment of only 150 per grade, about 500 more are on the drawing board.
3. And scores of online discussion boards have popped up on which people discuss negative experiences tied to too much time on the Web.
4. Joe is a day student, but I am a boarding student.

expire [ɪkˈspaɪə(r)] *v.* ①（of a document, an agreement, etc. 文件、协议等）to be no longer valid because the period of time for which it could be used has ended（因到期而）失效，终止；到期 ②（of a period of time, especially one during which sb. holds a position of authority 任期等）to end 届满

e.g. 1. When does your driving licence expire?

你的驾照什么时候到期？

e.g. 2. His term of office expires at the end of June.

他的任期六月底届满。

extol [ɪkˈstəʊl] *v.* (formal) to praise sb./sth. very much 赞扬；颂扬；称赞

e.g. 1. Doctors often extol the virtues of eating less fat.

医生常常宣扬少吃脂肪的好处。

e.g. 2. They kept extolling my managerial skills.

他们不停地赞美我的管理技能。

reflect on 仔细想；回忆；反省

e.g. I hope in years to come he will reflect on his decision.

我希望未来的几年里他会反省自己的决定。

turn out 结果是；关掉；制造；出席

e.g. Sometimes things don't turn out the way we think they're going to.

有时事情并不像我们认为的那样发展。

round the corner 在拐角处

e.g. I saw the car's nose appear round the corner.

scuttle off 跑掉；滚开

e.g. She scuttled off when she heard the sound of his voice.

听到他的说话声，她赶紧跑开了。

make it clear 使清楚

e.g. Be sure to make it clear and concise and avoid long-windedness.

注意简明扼要，反对长篇大论 .

Text B

Warming-up Activity:

Pre-reading Questions

1. Do you think it difficult for a woman to manage career-family balance at the same time?
2. In your opinion, when it comes to parenting, which is more important, quality or quantity?

The Other Choice Debate

It was not surprising when The New York Times ran an article about college women's talk on work-family balance a few weeks ago; the results, however, were a bit surprising. The article, "Many women at elite colleges choose career path to motherhood", profiled a number of young women who plan to opt out of the workforce once they have children. While this is not a new phenomenon, the article was disconcerting on several levels.

To begin with, almost all the students in the interview — and perhaps the author herself — seemed convinced that it is just too hard to manage a thriving career and a happy family at the same time. "My mother always told me you can't be the best career woman and the best mother ... You always have to choose one over the other." said one Yale sophomore. Choosing to stay at home with the kids is not a bad thing. Many women find motherhood to be the most fulfilling job there is. Yet others are not that interested in family at all. And then there is another group of women who would be fundamentally different, incomplete people without having jobs and children at the same time.

All these women exist today, and yet I wonder why more women of our generation do not realize the wealth of possibilities before them. Undeniably, problems still exist. For most professions, the most important years for building a career still coincide with women's prime childbearing years, and there does not seem to be a cure for working parents' guilt. But there is also progress. More men are opting to stay home to take care of kids while their wives go off to work. Many employers are beginning to offer — or even require — paternity leave for new fathers. Just this year, Princeton changed its policy for tenure track professors: all professors, male and female, are now automatically granted a tenure extension when they have a child. Employers can also provide affordable daycare and part-time work to accommodate new parents. For many jobs, having a phone and webmail at home is all employees need to get the job done. But we need to do a better job educating younger generations about all their options.

It is astounding that many young women do not realize that these choices exist. Yet even more alarming is the fact that some of the students in the article suggested that children of working mothers simply do not turn out as well as those who live with a stay-at-home mom: "I have seen the difference between kids who did have their mother stay at home and kids who did not, and it is kind of like an obvious difference when you look at it." said a freshman at the University of Pennsylvania. This statement is not just offensive to upper and middle class working mothers; it is an absolute affront to the many dedicated mothers who cannot afford to stay home with their children. In fact, many studies show that when it comes to parenting, it is not quantity, but quality that counts.

Many young women today need to be reassured that they can indeed work and have a family. Furthermore, we have to ask why it is that college-age women spend so much time grappling with the issue of work-family balance while their male classmates rarely give it a passing thought. There is nothing wrong with wanting to be a stay-at-home parent — what is wrong is that the parents who stay at home are disproportionately women.

There is no right way to manage a career and family, there is no sweeping prescription for everyone, and there is not necessarily one choice for an entire lifetime. There is a problem, though, with the fact that men do not seem to face these questions on the same level women do. Oddly, while women may be struggling with their choices, men may still not be fully aware of theirs.

The challenge — for men and women — is to figure out where we belong on the work-family spectrum. For some, the answer will be to take some time away from the time sheets and enjoy being a parent; others may find more satisfaction performing open heart surgery than applying band-aids; and some of us will get some twisted sense of pleasure from trying to manage both and feeling guilty all the time. What is important is that we understand that these options exist, and that we make sure they really are available to everyone. Rather than grading our choices, we need to look at the distribution of choice. Maybe this is simply a case of a reporter failing to tell all sides of the story. Maybe it is a larger problem in educating younger generations about all their career and family options. My only hope is that it is not a problem of these options being a fantasy. (815 words from *the Economist*)

Reading Exercises:

Check whether each statement is true (T) or false (F).

1. That a number of young women who plan to opt out of the workforce once they have children is a new phenomenon.
2. The author seemed agreed with that it is just too hard to manage a thriving career and a happy family at the same time.
3. More men are opting to stay home to take care of kids while their wives go off to work.
4. When it comes to parenting, it is not quality, but quantity that counts.
5. The challenge — for men and women — is to figure out where we belong on the work-family spectrum.

New Words and Phrases

Text B:

phenomenon[fəˈnɒminən] *n.* a fact or an event in nature or society, especially one that is not fully understood 现象 *pl.* phenomena

e.g. Globalization is a phenomenon of the 21st century.

全球化是 21 世纪的现象。

四级真题中的使用：

And most noticeable of all, there is the phenomenon of large urban and suburban high schools that have split up into smaller units of a few hundred, generally housed in the same grounds that once boasted thousands of students all marching to the same band.

thrive (in)[θraɪv] *v*. to become, and continue to be, successful, strong, healthy, etc. 兴旺发达；繁荣；蓬勃发展；旺盛；茁壮成长。派生词 thriving *adj*. 兴盛的

e.g. New business thrive in this area.

新商家在这一地区蓬勃兴起。

四级真题中的使用：

In the next couple of years the businesses that thrive will be those that are tight with costs, careful of debt, cautious with cash flow and extremely attentive to what customers want.

granted [ˈgrɑːntɪd] *v*. to agree to give sb. what they ask for, especially formal or legal permission to do sth.（退一步）承认（grant 的过去式和过去分词），（尤指正式的或法律上）同意；准许；让渡

e.g. The magistrates granted that the charity was justified in bringing the action.

地方法官承认该慈善机构有理由提起诉讼。

四级真题中的使用：

1. What is taken for granted by most people?
2. If you act like someone who expects a fair request to be granted, chances are it will be granted.

coincide with 与……一致

e.g. He happened to coincide with you on this point.

在这一问题上，他与你不谋而合。

tenure track 终身职位；终身聘用（尤其指大学任教）

e.g. It isn't a tenure track position but his contract can be renewed.

这不是一个终身职位，但他的合同可以续签。

grapple with 与……搏斗；竭力解决；努力克服

e.g. I've spent all afternoon grappling with these accounts.

我用了整整一下午处理这些账目。

struggle with 与……作斗争

e.g. Kenny, struggling with too many chairs, moved crabwise towards the door.

肯尼在许多椅子中间艰难穿行，像螃蟹一样横着向门口挪去。

Writing

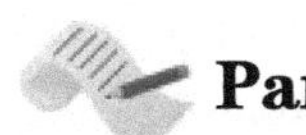

Part 1 命题分析

问题分析解决类

1. 定义

问题分析解决类作文要求考生针对给出的问题进行论述。题目所给的问题大多是当今社会的热门话题。通常要求考生分析问题产生的原因或危害，并提出解决问题的建议。

2. 写作步骤

基本提纲结构：第一段直击问题中心，用“一句话”来具体阐述和说明。第二、三段为对问题产生的原因或解决方法的分析，为文章的主体段落，要注意分层展开。

第一段：提出问题或现象。针对命题，概括性地提出所要论述的问题和现象的主要特点。

第二段：找出、分析问题的原因或后果。说明问题产生的原因是什么，并且要分析说明造成的后果是什么。

第三段：提出建议或解决问题的方法，或对目前无法解决的问题提出展望。

3. 问题分析解决类作文模板

问题分析解决类作文模版按照开头、正文和结尾三个部分呈现。

开头：

（1）It has now drawn（increasing public / much nationwide）attention to the (issue / problem) of _______.

（2）Currently, _________ has been brought to such popular attention that ________.

（3）According to (a survey / an investigation / a study / a poll), there is _________（提出问题）.

例：(Recently / Currently), the problem of global warming has been brought to such popular attention that governments at all levels place it on the top of the agenda.

According to the recent statistics, 80% teenagers are (addicted to / indulged in) playing online games.

正文：

（1）（分析原因）The (phenomenon / problem / failure / change) (of / in) ________ is (partly / mainly / largely) (attributable to.../due to.../owing to....) ________. First of all, _________. Secondly, ________. Finally, ______.

（2）（分析原因）There are (several / many / a number of / a variety of) (causes / reasons / factors) could (account for / contribute to / lead to) (the dramatic growth / extraordinary development / inevitable change) in ________.

（3）（分析影响或结果）：It is important for（people / teenagers）to realize that _________ will (produce / exert / have) a/an (remarkable / noticeable / striking / outstanding) (impact / influence / effect) on ________. In the first place, ________. In the second place, ________. Furthermore, __________.

结尾：

（1）There is (no denying/little doubt) that (special / adequate / considerable / further) attention must be (paid / called / devoted) to the problem of _________. If we (ignore / are blind to) the problem, it is very likely that ________.

（2）It is high time that strict measures were taken to _______. (It is time that we laid considerable special emphasis on the growth _______.)

（3）It is (suggested / recommended / hoped) that (great / persistent / continuous) efforts should _______. Anyhow, (wider education / more publicity) should be given to the serious (consequences / effects) of ________.

（4）Accordingly, it is imperative for us to take drastic measures. To begin with, we should (appeal to the authorities to make strict laws to ______). In addition, we should (cultivate the awareness of people that _______ is essential to us). Only in this way can we (reverse the disturbing trend illustrated above).

Part 2 练习

Directions: *For this part, you are allowed 30 minutes to write a composition on the topic **How to Deal with Sub-health**. You should write at least 120 words according to the outline given below in Chinese*:

1. 随着世界现代化的不断发展，人们的物质生活水平不断攀升，但人们却日益受到“亚健康”这种不良状态的威胁。

2. 亚健康的具体表现及在我国的蔓延程度（北京、上海、广州等地的上班族大都处于亚健康状态）。

3. 在现代社会中应怎样解决亚健康问题？

【审题】这道题要求考生谈如何解决亚健康问题，因此文章的体裁应该是议论文。文章的内容包括三个方面：一是亚健康问题的出现；二是亚健康问题的表现；三是如何解决亚健康问题。文章的重点应放在第二、三方面。文章的写作方向：亚健康问题的出现→亚健康表现为疲倦等→大多数上班族处于亚健康状态→缓解压力→拥有健康人生。

【中心思想】在物质生活水平不断提高的现代社会，亚健康问题出现了；具体表现为紧张、疲倦，身体状况不佳，多数上班族都处于亚健康状态；要解决亚健康问题，就要学会调整生活、缓解压力，以确保拥有健康的人生。

【写作提纲】

Para. 1: The appearance of sub-health problem

(1) Life of improved living standards

(2) The threat of sub-health

Para. 2: The symptoms and victims of sub-health

(1) The symptoms — fatigue, a sense of being ill

(2) The victims — office workers

Para. 3: The solution of the problem

(1) cause — quick pace of modern life

(2) solution — learning to slow down and enjoy life

【范文】

How to Deal with Sub-health

With the acceleration of global modernization, people are enjoying a constantly improved material life. At the same time, we may gradually find ourselves confronted with the threat of sub-health, a state between health and disease. Indeed, sub-health can result in both physical and mental diseases. Even worse, people who suffer from sub-health are more easily to die prematurely.

One typical symptom of sub-health is continual fatigue; the victim always feels tired and suspicious of some disease, which, however, is usually not to be detected through any physical check. Typical victim group consists of office workers, the active followers of material life yielded through their tense and hard work.

Considering the great harm brought by sub-health, I think it is high time that we took effective measures to prevent sub-health. As the quick pace of modern life is the ultimate cause of the problem, modern people had better learn to slow down a bit, try to do some exercise regularly to keep healthy. In addition, people must have enough sleep to ensure that they can regain energy and physical strength. To conclude, it is necessary for us to take flexible measures to avoid the threat of sub-health.

Vocabulary Exercises

A. *Fill in the blanks with the words in the box. Read the sentences carefully before making your choices. You may not use any of the words in the bank more than once. Change the form where necessary.*

associate	qualification	recruit	request	excessive	additional	rate	quotation
arrange	insure	specification	amount	comply	essence	principal	

1. Firms are now keen to hold on to the people they______.
2. The woman came to the concert at the man's______.
3. The police vigorously denied that______force had been used.
4. Shares and bonds can bring one quite a considerable______income.
5. They have only a vague idea of the______of water available.
6. He finished his speech with a______rom Shakespeare.
7. Speed was of the______in a project of this type.
8. The press feels the need to______itself with the green movement.
9. Think carefully before you______against accident, sickness and redundancy.
10. The Danube is one of the______rivers of Europe.

B. *Fill in the blanks with the phrases in the box. Read the sentences carefully before making your choices. You may not use any of the phrases in the bank more than once. Change the form where necessary.*

at any rate	commit to	comply with	as well as	qualify for	in excess	successful in
reward for	an amount of	associate with				

1. The commander said that the army would______the ceasefire.
2. Flowers are chosen for their scent______their look.
3. Well,______, let me thank you for all you did.
4. He advised his son never to spend______ of his income.
5. Mother warned the boys not to______bad companions.
6. You don't have to______anything over the phone.
7. She has been comparatively______maintaining her privacy.
8. He received a medal in______his bravery.
9. I have to do______homework every day.
10. The team failed to______the African Nations Cup finals.

Extended Exercises

Cloze

There is a passage with 10 blanks. You are required to select one word for each blank from a list of choices in a word bank following the passage. Read the passage through carefully before making your choices. Each choice in the bank is identified by a letter.

A) attendance	B) consequently	C) current	D) depressing
E) dropping	F) essential	G) feasible	H) flow
I) mood	J) mutually	K) particularly	L) performance
M) review	N) survive	O) tend	

Physical activity does the body good, and there's growing evidence that it helps the brain too. Researchers in the Netherlands report that children who get more exercise, whether at school or on their own, __1__ to have higher GPAs and better scores on standardized tests. In a __2__ of 14 studies that looked at physical activity and academic __3__ , investigators found that the more children moved, the better their grades were in school, __4__ in the basic subjects of math, English and reading.

The data will certainly fuel the ongoing debate over whether physical education classes should be cut as schools struggle to __5__ on smaller budgets. The arguments against physical education have included concerns that gym time may be taking away from study time. With standardized test scores in the U.S. __6__ in recent years, some administrators believe students need to spend more time in the classroom instead of on the playground. But as these findings show, exercise and academics may not be __7__ exclusive. Physical activity can improve blood __8__ to the brain, fueling memory, attention and creativity, which are __9__ to learning. And exercise releases hormones that can improve __10__ and relieve stress, which can also help learning. So while it may seem as if kids are just exercising their bodies when they're running around, they may actually be exercising their brains as well.

Paragraph Matching

You are going to read a passage with ten statements attached to it. Each statement contains information given in one of the paragraphs. Identify the paragraph from which the information is derived. You may choose a paragraph more than once. Each paragraph is marked with a letter.

[A] When your elderly relative needs to enter some sort of long-term care facility—a moment few parents or children approach without fear—what you would like is to have everything made clear.

[B] Does assisted living really mark a great improvement over a nursing home, or has the industry simply hired better interior designers? Are nursing homes as bad as people fear, or is that an out-moded stereotype（固定看法）? Can doing one's homework really steer families to the best places? It is genuinely hard to know.

[C] I am about to make things more complicated by suggesting that what kind of facility an older person lives in may matter less than we have assumed. And that the characteristics adult children look for when they begin the search are not necessarily the things that make a difference to the people who are going to move in. I am not talking about the quality of care, let me hastily add. Nobody flourishes in a gloomy environment with irresponsible staff and a poor safety record. But an accumulating body of research indicates that some distinctions between one type of elder care and another have little real bearing on how well residents do.

[D] The most recent of these studies, published in *The Journal of Applied Gerontology*, surveyed 150 Connecticut residents of assisted living, nursing homes and smaller residential care homes (known in some states as board and care homes or adult care homes). Researchers from the University of Connecticut Health Center asked the residents a large number of questions about their quality of life, emotional well-being and social interaction, as well as about the quality of the facilities.

[E] "We thought we would see differences based on the housing types." said the lead author of the study, Julie Robison, an associate professor of medicine at the university. A reasonable assumption— don't families struggle to avoid nursing homes and suffer real guilt if they can't?

[F] In the initial results, assisted living residents did paint the most positive picture. They were less likely to report symptoms of depression than those in the other facilities, for instance, and less likely to be bored or lonely. They scored higher on social interaction.

[G] But when the researchers plugged in a number of other variables, such differences disappeared. It is not the housing type, they found, that creates differences in residents' responses. "It is the characteristics of the specific environment they are in, combined with their own personal characteristics—how healthy they feel they are, their age and marital status." Dr. Robison explained. Whether residents felt involved in the decision to move and how long they had lived there also proved significant.

[H] An elderly person who describes herself as in poor health, therefore, might be no less depressed in assisted living (even if her children preferred it) than in a nursing home. A person who had input into where he would move and has had time to adapt to it might do as well in a nursing home as in a small residential care home, other factors being equal. It is an interaction between the person and the place, not the sort of place in itself, that leads to better or worse experiences. "You can't just say, 'Let's put this person in a residential care home instead of a nursing home—she will be much better off.'" Dr. Robison said. What matters, she added, "is a combination of what people bring in with them, and what they find there."

[I] Such findings, which run counter to common sense, have surfaced before. In a multi-state study of assisted living, for instance, University of North Carolina researchers found that a host of variables—the facility's type, size or age; whether a chain owned it; how attractive the neighborhood was—had no significant relationship to how the residents fared in terms of illness, mental decline, hospitalizations or mortality. What mattered most was the residents, physical health and mental status. What people were like when they came in had greater consequence than what happened once they were there.

[J] As I was considering all this, a press release from a respected research firm crossed my desk, announcing that the five-star rating system that Medicare developed in 2008 to help families compare nursing home quality also has little relationship to how satisfied its residents or their family members are. As a matter of fact, consumers expressed higher satisfaction with the one-star facilities, the lowest rated, than with the five-star ones. (More on this study and the star ratings will appear in a subsequent post.)

[K] Before we collectively tear our hair out—how are we supposed to find our way in a landscape this confusing?—here is a thought from Dr. Philip Sloane, a geriatrician（老年病学专家）at the University of North Carolina：“In a way, that could be liberating for families.”

[L] Of course, sons and daughters want to visit the facilities, talk to the administrators and residents and other families, and do everything possible to fulfill their duties. But perhaps they don't have to turn themselves into private investigators or Congressional subcommittees. "Families can look a bit more for where the residents are going to be happy." Dr. Sloane said. And involving the future resident in the process can be very important.

[M] We all have our own ideas about what would bring our parents happiness. They have their ideas, too. A friend recently took her mother to visit an expensive assisted living/nursing home near my town. I have seen this place—it is elegant, inside and out. But nobody greeted the daughter and mother when they arrived, though the visit had been planned; nobody introduced them to the other residents. When they had lunch in the dining room, they sat alone at a table.

[N] The daughter feared her mother would be ignored there, and so she decided to move her into a more welcoming facility. Based on what is emerging from some of this research, that might have been as rational a way as any to reach a decision.

1. Many people feel guilty when they cannot find a place other than a nursing home for their parents.
2. Though it helps for children to investigate care facilities, involving their parents in the decision-making process may prove very important.
3. It is really difficult to tell if assisted living is better than a nursing home.
4. How a resident feels depends on an interaction between themselves and the care facility they live in.
5. The author thinks her friend made a rational decision in choosing a more hospitable place over an apparently elegant assisted living home.
6. The system Medicare developed to rate nursing home quality is of little help to finding a satisfactory place.
7. At first the researchers of the most recent study found residents in assisted living facilities gave higher scores on social interaction.
8. What kind of care facility old people live in may be less important than we think.
9. The findings of the latest research were similar to an earlier multi-state study of assisted living.
10. A resident's satisfaction with a care facility has much to do with whether they had participated in the decision to move in and how long they had stayed there.

Cultural Translation

For this part, you are allowed 30 minutes to translate a passage from Chinese into English.

功夫（Kung Fu）是中国武术（martial arts）的俗称。中国武术的起源可以追溯到自卫的需要、狩猎活动以及古代中国的军事训练。它是中国传统体育运动的一种，年轻人和老年人都可以练。它已逐渐演变成了中国文化的特殊元素。功夫有上百种不同的风格，是世界上练得最多的武术形式。有些风格模仿了动物的动作，还有一些则受到了中国哲学思想、神话和传说的启发。

练习答案

Reading Exercises

Text A: 1 ～ 5 DACBD

Text B: 1 ～ 5 F T T F T

Vocabulary Exercises

A:

1. recruit
2. request
3. excessive
4. additional
5. amount
6. quotation
7. essence
8. associate
9. insure
10. principal

B:

1. comply with
2. as well as
3. at any rate
4. in excess
5. associate with
6. commit to
7. successful in
8. reward for
9. an amount of
10. qualify for

Extended Exercises

Cloze:

1 ～ 5: OMLKN　6 ～ 10: EJHFI

Paragraph Matching:

1 ～ 5: ELBHN　6 ～ 10: JFCIG

Cultural Translation:

Kung Fu is the folk name of Chinese martial arts, which can be traced back to the needs of self-defense, hunting, and military drill in ancient China. It is one of the Chinese traditional sports practiced by both the young and the old. It has gradually evolved into a unique element of Chinese culture. Kung Fu, as the national treasure of China, includes hundreds of various styles and is the most-practiced form of martial arts in the world. Some styles imitate the movements of animals, while others are inspired by Chinese philosophical thoughts, myths and legends.

Unit 2 My First Job

Learning Objectives

After completing this unit, you will be able to do the following:

◇ Practice for the skill: How to identify "the inverted pyramid structure";
◇ Grasp the main idea and the structure of the texts;
◇ Master the key language points and grammatical structure in the text;
◇ Conduct a series of reading, speaking and writing activities related to the theme in the unit.

Learning Difficult Points

In this unit, you will learn some difficult points listed below.
Listening: How to identify "the inverted pyramid structure".
Writing: Applied Writing

Outline

The Following are the main sections in this Unit.

1. Listening
2. Speaking
3. Reading: Text A & Text B
4. Writing
5. Extended Exercises

Vocabulary

Listed below are some words appearing in this unit that you should make part of your vocabulary.

eatery
shine
beam
pitch in
figure
promote
leverage
identical in
on average
amplified

Looking Ahead

My First Job

Every man's work, whether it be literature of music of pictures or architecture of anything else, is always a portrait of himself.

—Samuel Butler

Introduction

Yearly, numerous college graduates pour into job markets. As a result, some graduates easily win their job offers, while others fail in spite of sending resumes to many of their ideal companies. Then, "how to find a good job?" is a common question raised by college students.

The difficulties in seeking for good jobs are mainly as follows: First of all, a good position attracts talents in great numbers, which leads to an intense competition. Moreover, graduates swarm to the coastal cities, where the competition is fierce. Thirdly, plenty of companies request internship, which knocks many applicants out of the competition.

In college, students should try their best to gain more knowledge and competencies, and use them to arm themselves especially in these two aspects. At first, be proficient in English for most companies have a request for English. Students who possess an excellent spoken English capacity are possible to win a job in foreign-funded enterprises. Besides, gain specified certificates, which are needed for high-tech positions.

Speaking

Consider the following questions before reading:

1. What is your ideal job?
2. What is your job responsibility in your first job?

Conversation

Study and practice the conversation below.

A: Good morning. Is this the Student Job Centre?

B: Yes, it certainly is. How can I help you?

A: Well, actually I'm Looking for a job—a part-time job. Do you have anything available at the moment?

B: Ah..., yes.... Are you a registered student? I'm afraid this service is only available to full-time students.

A: Yes..., I am. I'm doing a degree in Business Studies. Here is my student card.

B: Which year are you in?

A: Well..., I've been at uni for four years, but I'm in the Third Years because I took last year off.

B: Ah, there's a job working at the reception desk at the Sports Center, for three evening a week— that's Wednesday, Thursdays and Friday.

A: En..., that's sounds like fun, Right....

B: OK, we'll fill in the personal detail on this application, if that's OK?

A: Yes, that's fine.

B: Would you like me to a arrange an interview for you? say, Friday morning, around ten?

A: Not a problem.

B: Hope it works out for you Anita.

A: Me too, And thanks for all your help.

UNIT 2 My First Job

Listening

Listening skills are fundamental to success in ENGLISH Listening. Through this part, we will have a detailed introduction to promote listening efficiency we could enhance by analyzing the three parts—News, Long conversation and Passage.

Listening Skills for News (2)

Keys to identify "the inverted pyramid structure"

Learn about "the inverted pyramid structure". News stories are organized in this structure, where information is presented in a descending order of the importance of the facts or the degree of concern people have about the issues. The top part represents the most important information that should head the article while the lower portion illustrates other facts in order of diminishing importance. "The inverted pyramid" is named for its structure which is as similar as an upside-down pyramid or a triangle.

Example（出自四级听力原文）

Three university students in Santiago, Chile, have developed a plant-powered device to charge their mobile phones.

智利圣地亚哥的三个大学生发明了能给手

导语（News Lead），它回答了 Who、Where、What 的问题，简明扼要地综述了新闻事件的要点。第 5 题可在导语中找到答案。

机充电的植物供能设备。

The three engineering students got the idea for the device while sitting in their school's courtyard.

这三个工程系学生是在学校操场上坐着的时候有的灵感。

Their invention is a small biological circuit they call E-Kaia.

他们的发明是一个小的生物电路，取名叫E-Kaia。

It captures the energy which plants produce during photosynthesis-a process of converting sunlight into energy.

当植物光合作用产能的时候，这个电路就会汲取能量。光合作用是把光能转化为植物自身的能量。

A plant uses only a small part of the energy produced by that process.

植物本身只会利用光合过程中的一小部分能量。

The rest goes into the soil.

其余的部分就进入了土壤。

E-Kaia collects that energy.

E-Kaia 就收集那一部分能量。

The device plugs into the ground and then into a mobile phone.

这个设备先插入土壤中然后再插入手机里。

The E-Kaia solved two problems for the engineering students.

新闻主体（Body），它介绍了细节 Where、How 的问题，第 6、7 题可在主体第一句中得到答案。

E-Kaia 为工程系学生解决了两个问题。

They needed an idea for a class project.

他们的这个灵感用于课堂项目。

They also needed an outlet to plug in their phones.

他们同时也需要有个地方插手机。

One of the student inventors, Camila Rupcich, says the device changes the energy released from the plant into low-level power to charge phones.

发明者之一的 Camila Rupcich 说，这个设备把植物释放的能量转换成较低的水平从而为手机充电。

The E-Kaia is able to fully recharge a mobile phone in less than two hours.

E-Kaia 能在两小时内把手机充满电。

Questions 5 to 7 are based on the news report you have just heard.

请根据你刚刚听到的新闻报道回答问题 5 至问题 7。

Question 5. What did the three university students invent?

问题 5. 三个大学生发明了什么？

Question 6. When did they get the idea for the invention?

问题 6. 他们什么时候有的灵感？

Question 7. What does the speaker say about the invention?

问题 7. 说话的人怎么评价这个发明？

Reading

Text A

Warming-up Activity:

Being proud of your job is part of your commitment to your work which may be in the form of mopping clean floors or managing a large business. Anyway, you are a valuable person, which is unrelated to whatever job you have chosen for your career, how much money you have earned in your bank account or whatever kind of car you have bought. In a word, you are important and that is enough.

My First Job

My parents ran the Pagonis Restaurant, a small eatery in Charleroi, pa. The Pagonis was open 24 hours a day, seven days a week, and my first real job, when I was six years old, was shinning dinners' shoes. My father had done it when he was young, so he taught me how to do it right, telling me to ask the customer if I'd done a good job and to offer to reshine the shoes if the customer was not satisfied.

My duties increased as I grew older. By age ten, I was clearing tables and working as the janitor. Dad beamed when he told me that I was the best "mop guy" he'd ever had.

Working in the restaurant was a source of great pride because I was pitching in for the good of the whole family. But my father made it clear I had to meet certain standards to be part of the team. I had to be punctual, hard working,and polite to the customers.

Except the shoe shinning job, I was never paid for any work I did at the restaurant. One day I made the mistake of telling dad that I thought he should give me $10 a week. He said, "okay, then how about you paying me for the three meals a day you eat here? And for the times you bring in your buddies for free sodas? " He figured I owed him about $40 a week. This taught me that when you negotiate, you'd better know the other side's arguments as well as your own.

I remember coming home to Charleroi after being away in the Army about two years. I had just been promoted to captain and was full of pride as I walked into my parents' restaurant. The first thing dad said was, "it's the janitor' day off. How about you cleaning up tonight?" I can't believe this! I thought. I am an officer in the United States Army! But it didn't matter. As far as dad was concerned, I was just another member of the team. I reached for the mop.

Working for dad had taught me that loyalty to the team comes first. It doesn't matter whether that team is involved in a family or Operation Desert Storm.

Reading Exercises:

1. What does this passage mainly tell us?

A. The most important quality that one needs is to do a good job.

B. The author used to work as a janitor in the Pagonis Restaurant.

C. Some parents pay their children for the work they have done for the family.

D. Parents should not pay their children for the work they have done for the family.

2. What was the author's first job?

A. His first job was clearing tables and working as the janitor.

B. He served as a waiter serving dishes.

C. His first job was shining diners' shoes.

D. He was an officer in the United States Army.

3. Which of the following statements is NOT true ?

A. His parents ran the Pagonis Restaurant, a small eatery in Charleroi, pa.

B. His father taught him how to do it right, telling him to ask the customer if he'd done a good job.

C. By age ten, he was clearing tables and working as the janitor.

D. He got fewer duties when he grew older.

4. What are the certain standards that his father made clear?

A. To be part of the team.

B. To be punctual.

C. To be polite with the customers.

D.A, B, and C.

5. What kind of reception did the narrator get when he returned home?

A.His father asked him to shine diner's shoes.

B.His father asked him to clean up.

C.His father asked him to have a good rest.

D.His parents welcomed him to get back to the team.

New Words and Phrases

Text A:

eatery [ˈi:təri] *n.*〔美〕餐馆，食堂；

e.g. We met in a little eatery just off the main road.

我们在主路旁的小餐馆见面。

shine〔英〕[ʃaɪn] *v.* 发出光；反射光，闪耀；出类拔萃，表现突出；露出

e.g. The sun shone brightly in a cloudless sky.

太阳在无云的天空中明亮地照耀着。

beam [bi:m] *n.* 梁，栋梁；束；光线；*vi.* 发出光与热；面露喜色；

e.g. 1. She froze when the beam of the flashlight struck her.

当手电筒的光照到她身上时她僵住了。

e.g. 2. His father beamed with satisfaction.

他爸爸眉开眼笑地表示满意。

pitch in 动手干，作贡献

e.g. You should pitch in if you want to win success.
如果你想成功就要努力。

figure [ˈfɪgə(r)] *n.* 数字；算术；人物；身材 *v.* 计算在内；估计；推测；认为

e.g. Just when you had figured out how to manage fat in your diet, researchers are now warning against another common mealtime pitfall— salt.
当你已经了解了如何在日常饮食中控制脂肪、胆固醇以及转化脂肪的时候，研究者现在对另一个日常食谱中的陷阱提出了警告——盐。

四级真题中的使用：

SAT scores began dropping in 1963; today, on average, 30% of students do not complete high school in four years, a figure that rises to 50% in poor urban neighborhoods.

promote [prəˈməʊt] *v.* 促进，推进；提升

e.g. Do you have any idea how to promote the sales of this product?
如何来推销这种产品你有什么好办法吗？

四级真题中的使用：

1. The question of whether our government should promote science and technology or the liberal arts in higher education isn't an either/or proposition(命题),although the current emphasis on preparing young Americans for STEM (science, technology, engineering, maths)-related fields can make it seem that way.
2. Politicians who thoughtlessly promoted home-ownership for those who could not afford it?

negotiate [nɪˈgəʊʃieɪt] *v.* 谈判，协商

e.g. Western governments have this week urged him to negotiate and avoid force.
西方各国政府本周敦促他进行谈判，避免使用武力。

四级真题中的使用：

1. He said the report was aimed at world leaders, who will meet in Copenhagen in December to negotiate a new international climate treaty.
2. Industrial scientists tend to receive training that academics do not, such as how to build a multidisciplinary team, manage budgets and negotiate contracts.

loyalty [ˈlɔɪəlti] *n.* 忠诚，忠实；忠心；忠于……感情

e.g. 1. There were too many other demands on his loyalty now.

现在还有太多其他的事情也要求他忠心。

e.g. 2. But what was perhaps most astonishing about Mr. Jobs was the absolute loyalty he managed to inspire in customers.

所以乔布斯成功最令人震惊的地方在于他获得了苹果用户的绝对忠诚。

except for 除……之外；若不是

e.g. Except for the remarkably tidy kitchen, the place was a mess.

除了厨房特别干净外，这地方一片狼藉。

have/take a day off (not to work for a day) 放假一天

e.g. Can I have a day off?

我能请一天假吗？

As/so far as ... be concerned 我认为；对我来说

e.g. As far as I am concerned the matter is closed.

对我来说，事情已了结 .

Text B

Warming-up Activity:

Pre-reading Questions

1. What qualities do you think are important to achieve success?

2. How can a person persuade his employer that he is suitable for the job?

Contact Sports

Abbreviated from *The Economist*

Women are worse than men at turning networks to their advantage IN THE rarefied world of the corporate board, a good network matters. Recruitment often involves word-of-mouth recommendations: getting on a shortlist is easier if you have the right connections. New research suggests men use contacts better than women.

Marie Lalanne and Paul Seabright of the Toulouse School of Economics measure the effect of a network on remuneration using a database of board members in Europe and America. They find that if you were to compare two executive directors, identical in every way except that one had 200 ex-colleagues now sitting on boards and the other 400, the latter, on average, would be paid 6% more. For non-executives the gap is 14%.

The really juicy finding concerns the difference between the sexes. Among executive-board members, women earn 17% less than their male counterparts. There are plenty of plausible explanations for this disparity, from interruptions to women's careers to old-fashioned discrimination. But the authors find that this pay gap can be fully explained by the effect of executives' networks. Men can leverage a large network into more senior positions or a seat on a more lucrative board; women don't seem to be able to.

Women could just have weaker connections with members of their networks. "Women seem more inclined to build and rely on only a few strong relationships." says Mr. Seabright. Men are better at developing passing acquaintances into a network, and better at maintaining a high personal profile through these contacts. Women may, of course, also be hurt by the existing dominance of men on boards and a male preference for filling executive positions with other men. But a tendency to think of other men first will be amplified if talented women don't stay on the radar.

Interestingly, there is only a marginal pay difference between men and women when it comes to non-executive directors, and no difference in the effectiveness of their networks. It is possible that this reflects pressure for "gender quotas" on corporate boards. Women are able to find their way onto shortlists for lower-paid, non-executive positions. But that's not where the real power lies.

Reading Exercises:

Check whether each statement is true (T) or false (F).

According to the article, determine whether the following statements are true or false.

1. By studying the impact of social connections on pay, they found that men in comparable positions were paid 17% more than women in non-executives.
2. Compared with men, women are completely unable to leverage a large network into more senior positions or a seat on a more lucrative board.
3. Although men are better at building passing acquaintances into a network, they are less active in these contacts.
4. The study found that even though women can get jobs by accepting lower pay or entering non-executive areas, which is not the result of the optimal allocation of resources.
5. Recent research shows that women are less adept at using their interpersonal relationships.

New Words and Phrases

Text B:

corporate [ˈkɔːpərət] *adj.* ① forming a corporation 组成公司（或团体）的；法人的 ② involving or shared by all the members of a group 社团的；全体的；共同的

e.g. The law applies to both individuals and corporate bodies.

本法律既适用于个人也适用于法人团体。

四级真题中的使用：

1. Within the wider business world, a man who liked to see himself as a hippy（嬉皮士）, permanently in revolt against big companies, ended up being hailed by many of those corporate giants as one of the greatest chief executives of his time.
2. As our special report in this issue (printed before Mr. Jobs's death) explains, innovation used to spill over from military and corporate laboratories to the

consumer market, but lately this process has gone into reverse.

recruitment [rɪˈkru:tmənt] *n.* 征募新兵；补充；招聘

e.g. We're going to launch a big recruitment drive in autumn.

我们将在秋季进行大规模征兵。

remuneration [rɪˌmju:nəˈreɪʃn] *n.* an amount of money that is paid to sb. for the work they have done 酬金；薪水；报酬

e.g. He received a generous remuneration for his services.

他收到一笔丰厚的劳务酬金。

disparity [dɪˈspærəti] *n.* a difference, especially one connected with unfair treatment（尤指因不公正对待引起的）不同，不等，差异，悬殊

e.g. The disparity in incomes among different professions was small.

各职业收入的差距比较小。

四级真题中的使用：

This disparity（差异）suggests the memory of our previous meal may have a bigger influence on our appetite than the actual size of the meal.

discrimination [dɪˌskrɪmɪˈneɪʃn] *n.* the practice of treating sb. or a particular group in society less fairly than others 区别对待；歧视；偏袒

e.g. They focus on overt discrimination rather than insidious aspects of racism.

他们关注的是公开的歧视，而不是种族主义的一些潜在问题。

leverage [ˈli:vərɪdʒ] *n.* ① the ability to influence the ability to influence situations or people so that you can control what happens 影响力，手段，优势 ②杠杆作用；杠杆效力

e.g. He has some leverage over the politician.

他对这位政界人士有些影响。

profile [ˈprəʊfaɪl] *v.* to give or write a description of sb./sth. that gives the most important information 扼要介绍；概述；写简介 *n.* a description of sb./sth. that gives useful information 概述；简介；传略 the edge or outline of sth. that you see against a background 外形；轮廓

e.g. We first build up a detailed profile of our customers and their requirements.

首先，我们建立起我们的客户及其需求的详细资料。

amplify[ˈæmplɪfaɪ] *v.* ① to increase sth. in strength, especially sound 放大，增强

（声音等）② to add details to a story, statement, etc. 详述，充实（故事、事情、陈述等）*n.* amplification

e.g. He amplified on his remarks with drawings and figures.

他用图表详细地解释了他的话。

identical in 相同

e.g. He is identical in character with his wife. 他的品性和他的夫人相同。

on average 平均

e.g. American shares rose, on average, by 38%.

美国股票价格平均上涨了 38%。

inclined to 倾向于

e.g. Henry was inclined to seek solace in drink.

亨利往往借酒消愁。

stay on 留下来继续（学习、工作等）

e.g. He expects me to stay on here and I can hardly refuse.

他希望我继续留在这里，我很难拒绝。

when it comes to 当涉及某事（或做某事）时

e.g. They don't accept any foolishness when it comes to spending money.

在花钱的问题上，他们向来很谨慎。

Writing

Part 1 命题分析

比较对照、选择类

1. 定义

对比选择类文章，要求考生就题目中提到的某一事物或社会现象给出两个对立的观点，然后将两种观点进行对比，并表明自己的看法和立场，或作出选择。所提出的两种观点有时并没有对错之分，有时也可以根据常识判断出某一观点错误或者不成立。

2. 写作步骤

题型	第一段	第二段	第三段
对比选择	表明一方或双方的观点	表明另一方的观点及理由，或指出双方观点的不足及理由	表明个人的观点或阐述个人的做法

题型	文章线索	组材方法
对比选择	权衡两种不同方法或观点的利弊	（1）分析观点一的利弊 — 观点二的利弊— 作出最佳选择； （2）两观点各自的优点— 各自的不足—作出选择

3. 对比选择型作文模板

模板一：

There is no complete agreement among people as to ______. Some people consider that ______. However, others think that ______.

Some people contend that ______. They hold this opinion because ______. However, others who stand on a different ground believe that ______. They argue that ______.

Personally, I prefer the former/latter opinion/choice. Firstly, ______. Secondly, ______. Most important of all, ______. Taking the above-mentioned into consideration, we/I may reasonably conclude that______.

模板二：

When asked about / When it comes to ______, different people will offer different opinions. Some people take it for granted that ______. In their opinion, ______. Besides, ______.

By contrast, others hold that ______. They maintain that ______. And ______.

Weighing up these two arguments, I am for the first opinion/choice. For one thing/ On the one hand, ______ For another / On the other hand, ______. For instance, ______. Therefore, as stated above, ______.

Part 2 练习

Directions: *For this part, you are allowed 30 minutes to write a composition on the topic* ***High Salaries or Career Development****? You should write at least 150 words, and base your composition on the outline (given in Chinese) below*:

（1）有的大学毕业生选择工作时主要看重高工资，而有的则认为良好的职业发展空间才是更重要的；

（2）阐述他们各自的考虑；

（3）表明你的看法。

【行文思路】

本题属于提纲式文字命题。提纲第 1 点指出两种不同的选择，提纲第 2 点要求分别阐述这两种选择各自的理由，提纲第 3 点要求表明“我”的看法。由此可判断，本文应为对比选择型作文。

根据所给提纲，本文应包含如下内容：指出大学毕业生选择工作时不同的侧重点：注重高工资和注重职业发展空间，对比阐述他们各自的理由，表明“我”的倾向并说明理由。

【范文】

High Salaries or Career Development?

There are more and more people looking for jobs every year, but they have different views about what kind of job they should choose. Some of them focus their attention on the jobs that promise high salaries. Others show a preference for those jobs that offer chances to learn skills and advancement possibilities.

People holding the first view usually think that more money will result in more happiness. With a lot of money in hand, they will be able to enjoy a rich life. Otherwise, they will suffer from depression due to lack of enough money. However, the holders of the second view argue that one should develop his skills as roundly as possible. It is career development that counts most. Without development, you will be outrun by others and fall behind the times sooner or later.

In my view, career development is the right choice because career may give us long term satisfaction while high salary would give us short term happiness. Besides, generally speaking, a good career development will bring high salaries sooner or later. So I will give my vote to the career development first and then high salaries.

Vocabulary Exercises

A. *Fill in the blanks with the words in the box. Read the sentences carefully before making your choices. You may not use any of the words in the bank more than once. Change the form where necessary.*

shine promote recruitment corporate disparity amplify loyalty negotiate remuneration profile leverage discrimination

1. The owner opened a ________ checking account at the bank.
2. Other possible applications would be on dating websites or in ________ .
3. He objected to receive any ________ for his service .
4. There is a great ________ in strength between the two teams.
5. ________ against Blacks still exists in America.
6. We can lift extremely heavy things by ________ .
7. We could see the ________ of a distant hill if it is very clear.
8. The music was ________ with microphones.
9. I managed ________ successfully with the authorities.
10. Despite her sharp tongue, she inspires ________ from her friends.
11. Charles has been ________ to general sales and marketing manager.
12. The container is invisible until you ________ an ultraviolet light on it.

B. *Fill in the blanks with the phrases in the box. Read the sentences carefully before making your choices. You may not use any of the phrases in the bank more than once. Change the form where necessary.*

identical in how about stay on have a day off when it comes to inclined to on average except for pitch in figure up

1. These two words are ________ meaning and can be used interchangeably.
2. ________ he watches three movies a week.

3. She has always been __________ excitability.
4. So few teenage Britons __________ at school, compared with the rest of Europe.
5. __________ music, I'm a complete ignoramus.
6. __________ going shopping and seeing a show in London?
7. The foggy streets were virtually empty, __________the occasional evening stroller.
8. The agency says international relief agencies also have __________.
9. The cook is __________ today.
10. He __________ the balance in their checking account.

Extended Exercises

Cloze

There is a passage with 10 blanks. You are required to select one word for each blank from a list of choices in a word bank following the passage. Read the passage through carefully before making your choices. Each choice in the bank is identified by a letter.

A) dependent	B) designed	C) fast	D) flying
E) gained	F) give	G) growing	H) launch
I) policy	J) prospect	K) rather	L) reliable
M) signal	N) successful	O) treatments	

Signs barring cell-phone use are a familiar sight to anyone who has ever sat in a hospital waiting room. But the __1__ popularity of electronic medical records has forced hospital-based doctors to become __2__ on computers throughout the day, and desktops—which keep doctors from bedsides— are __3__ giving way to wireless devices.

As clerical loads increased, "something had to __4__ , and that was always face time with patients." says Dr. Bhakti Patel, a former chief resident in the University of Chicago's internal-medicine program. In fall 2010, she helped __5__ a pilot project in Chicago to see if the iPad could improve working conditions and patient care. The experiment was so __6__ that all internal-medicine residents at the university now get iPads when they begin the program. Johns Hopkins, internal-medicine program adopted the same ___7___ in 2011. Medical schools at Yale and Stanford now have paperless, iPad-based curriculums. "You'll want an iPad just so you can wear this" is the slogan for one of the new lab coats ___8___ with large pockets to accommodate tablet computers.

A study of the University of Chicago iPad project found that patients got tests and ___9___ faster if they were cared for by iPad-equipped residents. Many patients also ___10___ a better understanding of the illnesses that landed them in the hospital in the first place.

Paragraph Matching

You are going to read a passage with ten statements attached to it. Each statement contains information given in one of the paragraphs. Identify the paragraph from which the information is derived. You may choose a paragraph more than once. Each paragraph is marked with a letter.

[A] Is it possible to enjoy a peaceful life in a world that is increasingly challenged by threats and uncertainties from wars, terrorism, economic crises and a widespread outbreak of infectious diseases? The answer is yes, according to a new book *The 10 Golden Rules: Ancient Wisdom from the Greek Philosophers on Living a Good Life*. The book is co-authored by Long Island University's philosophy professor Michael Soupios and economics professor Panos Mourdoukoutas.

[B] The wisdom of the ancient Greek philosophers is timeless, says Soupios. The philosophy professor says it is as relevant today as when it was first written centuries ago. "There is no expiration（失效）date on wisdom." he says. "There is no shelf life on intelligence. I think that things have become very gloomy these days, lots of misunderstanding, misleading cues, a lot of what the ancients would have called sophistry（诡辩）. The nice thing about ancient philosophy as offered by the Greeks is that they tended to see life clear and whole, in a way that we tend not to see life today."

[C] Soupios, along with his co-author Panos Mourdoukoutas, developed their 10 golden rules by turning to the men behind that philosophy—Aristotle, Socrates, Epictetus and Pythagoras, among others. The first rule—examine your life—is the common thread that runs through the entire book. Soupios says that it is based on Plato's observation that the unexamined life is not worth living. "The Greeks are always concerned about boxing themselves in, in terms of convictions（信念）." he says. "So take a step back, switch off the automatic pilot and actually stop and reflect about things like our priorities, our values, and our relationships."

[D] As we begin to examine our life, Soupios says, we come to Rule No. 2: Worry only about things that you can control. "The individual who promoted this idea was a Stoic philosopher. His name is Epictetus." he says. "And what the Stoics say in general is simply this: There is a larger plan in life. You are not really going to be able to understand all of the dimensions of this plan. You are not going to be able to control the dimensions of this plan."

[E] So, Soupios explains, it is not worth it to waste our physical, intellectual and spiritual energy worrying about things that are beyond our control. "I can not control whether or not I wind up getting the disease swine flu, for example." he says. "I mean, there are some cautious steps I can take, but ultimately I can not guarantee myself that. So what Epictetus would say is sitting at home worrying about that would be wrong and wasteful and irrational. You should live your life attempting to identify and control those things which you can genuinely control."

[F] To have a meaningful, happy life we need friends. But according to Aristotle—a student of Plato and teacher of Alexander the Great—most relationships don't qualify as true friendships. "Just because I have a business relationship with an individual and I can profit from that relationship, it does not necessarily mean that this person is my friend." Soupios says. "Real friendship is when two individuals share the same soul. It is a beautiful and uncharacteristically poetic image that Aristotle offers."

[G] In our pursuit of the good life, he says, it is important to seek out true pleasures—advice which was originally offered by Epicurus. But unlike the modern definition of Epicureanism as a life of indulgence（放纵）and luxury, for the ancient Greeks, it meant finding a state of calm, peace and mental ease.

[H] "This was the highest and most desirable form of pleasure and happiness for the ancient Epicureans." Soupios says. "This is something that is very much well-worth considering here in the modern era. I do not think that we spend nearly enough time trying to concentrate on achieving a sort of calmness, a sort of contentment in a mental and spiritual way, which was identified by these people as the highest form of happiness and pleasure."

[I] Other Golden Rules counsel us to master ourselves, to avoid excess and not to be a prosperous（发迹的）fool. There are also rules dealing with interpersonal relationships: Be a responsible human being and do not do evil things to others.

[J] "This is Hesiod, of course, a younger contemporary poet, we believe, with Homer." Soupios says. "Hesiod offers an idea—which you very often find in some of the world's great religions, in the Judeo-Christian tradition and in Islam and others—that in some sense, when you hurt another human being, you hurt yourself. That damaging other people in your community and in your life, trashing relationships, results in a kind of self-inflicted（自己招致的）spiritual wound."

[K] Instead, Soupios says, ancient wisdom urges us to do good. Golden Rule No. 10 for a good life is that kindness toward others tends to be rewarded.

[L] "This is Aesop, the fabulist（寓言家）, the man of these charming little tales, often told in terms of animals and animal relationships." he says. "I think what Aesop was suggesting is that when you offer a good turn to another human being, one can hope that good deed will come back and sort of pay a profit to you, the doer of the good deed. Even if there is no concrete benefit paid in response to your good deed, at the very least, the doer of the good deed has the opportunity to enjoy a kind of spiritually enlightened moment."

[M] Soupios says following the 10 Golden Rules based on ancient wisdom can guide us to the path of the good life where we stop living as onlookers and become engaged and happier human beings. And that, he notes, is a life worth living.

1. According to an ancient Greek philosopher, it is impossible for us to understand every aspect of our life.
2. Ancient philosophers saw life in a different light from people of today.
3. Not all your business partners are your soul mates.
4. We can live a peaceful life despite the various challenges of the modern world.
5. The doer of a good deed can feel spiritually rewarded even when they gain no concrete benefits.
6. How to achieve mental calmness and contentment is well worth our consideration today.
7. Michael Soupios suggests that we should stop and think carefully about our priorities in life.
8. Ancient philosophers strongly advise that we do good.
9. The wise teachings of ancient Greek thinkers are timeless, and are applicable to contemporary life.
10. Do harm to others and you do harm to yourself.

Cultural Translation

Directions: *For this part, you are allowed 30 minutes to translate a passage from Chinese into English.*

在山东省潍坊市，风筝不仅是玩具，而且还是这座城市文化的标志。潍坊因“风筝之都”闻名，已有将近 2400 年制作风筝的历史。传说中国古代哲学家墨子用了三年时间在潍坊制作了世界上首个风筝，但放飞的第一天风筝就坠落并摔坏了。也有人相信风筝是中国古代木匠鲁班发明的。据说他的风筝用木头和竹子制作，飞了三天后才落地。

练习答案

Reading Exercises

Text A: 1 ～ 5 ACDDB

Text B: 1 ～ 5 FFFTT

Vocabulary Exercises

A:

1. corporate
2. recruitment
3. remuneration
4. disparity
5. Discrimination
6. leverage
7. profile
8. amplified
9. to negotiate
10. loyalty
11. promoted
12. shine

B:

1. identical in
2. On average
3. inclined to
4. stay on
5. When it comes to
6. How about
7. except for
8. pitched in
9. having a day off
10. figured up

Extended Exercises

Cloze:

1 ～ 10: GACFH NIBOE

Paragraph Matching:

1 ～ 10: DBFAL HCKBJ

Cultural Translation:

In the Weifang City of Shandong Province, kites are more than toys; they are also the cultural symbol of the city. Known as "Kite Capital of the World", Weifang has had a history of kite-flying of nearly 2400 years. Legend has it that Mozi, an ancient Chinese philosopher, spent three years making the first kite of the world in Weifang, but the kite fell and broke on its first day of flying. It is also believed that the kite was invented by the ancient Chinese carpenter Lu Ban. It is said that his kite, made of wood and bamboo, had been flying in the sky for three days before falling to the ground.

Unit 3 Art and Tourism

Learning Objectives

After completing this unit, you will be able to do the following:

◇ Practice for the skill: How to predict;

◇ Grasp the main idea and the structure of the texts;

◇ Master the key language points and grammatical structure in the text;

◇ Conduct a series of reading, speaking and writing activities related to the theme in the unit.

Learning Difficult Points

In this unit, you will learn some difficult points listed below.

◇ Listening: How to predict.

◇ Writing: Applied Writing

Outline

The Following are the main sections in this Unit.

1. Listening
2. Speaking
3. Reading: Text A & Text B
4. Writing
5. Extended Exercises

Vocabulary

Listed below are some words appearing in this unit that you should make part of your vocabulary.

sculpting
cartography
deciphering
contention
breakthrough
monumental
contribute to
be fascinated by
take into account

Looking Ahead

Art and Tourism

Works of art, in my opinion, are the only objects in the material universe to possess internal order, and that is why, though I don't believe that only art matters, I do believe in Art for Art's sake.

—E. M. Forster

Introduction

Harbin's Tourism Project: International Ice Festival

Today, Harbin Ice Festival is not only an exposition of ice and snow art, but also an annual cultural event for international exchange. Every year, there are many ice sculpture experts, artists and fans from America, Canada, Japan, Singapore, Russia, China, etc. gathering in Harbin to participate ice sculpting competitions and to communicate with each other in the ice and snow world. Also, Harbin ice lanterns have been exhibited in most of China's main cities as well as in many countries in Asia, Europe, North America, Africa and Oceania. For more than 40 years, Harbin's natural resource of ice and snow has been fully explored to provide joy and fun for visitors to the city. Now during the festival, many sporting competitions are also popular including ice-skating, sledding and so on. Weddings, parties and other entertainments are now very much a feature of this ice world , adding their own contribution to the celebrations of this great festival of art, culture, sports and tourism.

Speaking

Consider the following questions before reading:

1. Do you like painting? Do you think art plays an important role in society?
2. Do you think it's possible for everyone to become an artist?

Conversation

Role-play. Talk about your understanding of art.

A: Shona, do you consider yourself an artist?

B: No, actually, I wouldn't use that word.

A: I don't like when people use that word, cause artist to me is someone who is famous for creating something, being a creator or a designer. but I do like sort of things, so I like to paint and I like to draw and I like to create things and design things.

B: So what kind of things do you like to paint?

A: I like kind of all forms of art really. OK, well, the kind of paintings I do are based on two things I've noticed over this time that I've been doing it—Color and shape.

UNIT 3 Art and Tourism

Listening

Listening skills are fundamental to success in ENGLISH Listening. Through this part, we will have a detailed introduction to promote listening efficiency we could enhance by analyzing the three parts—News, Long conversation and Passage.

Listening Skills for Long Conversation (1)

Predicting

There are many skills in listening and understanding long conversations. One tip is to warm up and predict what the questions may be, collecting the information which is related to one of the four choices while listening. If you have trouble guessing the questions, consider the major question words 5Ws, and a how-who, when, where, which, what and how, which leads you to get the context earlier.

For example, when the four choices are as follows:

A) In the morning; B) In the afternoon; C) In the evening; D) At midnight.

Then it can be referred that the question may talk about time when the conversation happens or when an event takes place.

Here is another example.

A) Doctor; B) Journalist; C) Writer; D) Traveler.

It's no denying that the question is concerned with someone's occupation which will be discussed in the long conversation. Then concentrate more on the places and terms they refer to.

Example（出自四级听力原文）

Question 8

A) He's got addicted to technology.

B) He is not very good at socializing.

C) He is crazy about text-messaging.

D) He does not talk long on the phone.

Question 9

A) Talk big.

B) Talk at length.

C) Gossip a lot.

D) Forget herself.

Question 10

A) He thought it was cool.

B) He needed the practice.

C) He wanted to stay connected with them.

D) He had an urgent message to send.

Question 11

A) It poses a challenge to seniors.

B) It saves both time and money.

C) It is childish and unprofessional.

D) It is cool and convenient.

M: So, Linzy, do you like to text message on your cell phone?

On a basis of what has been mentioned above, in order to copy with the difficult listening materials, it is useful to warm the answers up and make a prediction about the questions.

In this long conversation, the repeated words "message", "talk", indicate that the main idea should be connected with messaging on phone.

The repeated word "He" 简明地告知此题考查的是说话人的态度。

W: Yeah, I text message a lot.

M: I don't do it so much. I prefer to make a call if I'm in a hurry.

W: Yeah, I go both ways. Sometimes I don't really want to talk to the person. I just want to ask them one question, so it's much easier for me just to text message. If I call them, I'll have to have a long conversation.

M: Yeah, I can see what you mean. But I get off the phone pretty quickly when I call. I'm not a big talker.

W: Yeah, that's true. You don't talk a lot.

M: So are you fast at writing the messages with your thumb?

W: Well, when I first got a cell phone, I was so slow. I thought I would never text message. But then people kept text messaging me, so I felt obliged to learn how to text message. So now I'm pretty fast. What about you?

M: Actually I have the opposite problem. When I first got my cell phone, I thought it was so cool to text message to all my friends who have one, and I was pretty fast with my thumb then. But it seems like now I don't use it so much, I've got slower actually.

W: Yeah, I think text messaging actually is what you have to do with your age. For example, people in high school, they text message a lot. But I ask my father if he texted messages, and guess what he said?

M: What?

W: He said he'd never text message. He thinks it's very childish and unprofessional to text message.

M: Yeah, I can see what he means. It's considered pretty informal to text message to someone.

Questions 8 to 11 are based on the conversation you've just heard.

Q8: What does the man say about himsclf?

Q9: What does the woman tend to do while she is on the phone?

Q10: Why did the man text message to all his friends when he first got his cell phone?

Q11: What does the woman's father think of text messaging?

这篇新闻中，"message""talk""he"等词语在选项中重复使用，给出文章线索，为理解对话内容打下基础。因此，抓住已知提示进行题目预测很重要。

Reading

Text A

Warming-up Activity:

Leonardo di ser Piero da Vinci (Italian, 15 April 1452—2 May 1519), more commonly Leonardo da Vinci or simply Leonardo, was an Italian Renaissance polymath whose areas of interest included invention, painting, sculpting, architecture, science, music, mathematics, engineering, literature, anatomy, geology, astronomy, botany, writing, history, and cartography. He has been variously called the father of palaeontology, ichnology, and architecture, and is widely considered one of the greatest painters of all time.

Leonardo in London
Deciphering the da Vinci Code

—Abbreviated from *The Economist*

A new show offers a rare opportunity to compare Leonardo da Vinci's paintings.

SCIENTIST, engineer, musician and great artist, Leonardo da Vinci is the archetypal Renaissance man. This undisputed genius, who lived to be 67, also one of history's most accomplished underachievers. He started many projects he did not finish; he accepted commissions he never began; his many planned treatises remained just notes. Only 18 of his paintings survive. Half of them are included in a show that opened on November 9th at London's National Gallery, making this the most important da Vinci display ever.

The artist was born near Florence in 1452 and went to Milan at the age of 30. Luke Syson, the show's curator, has come to believe that the freedom da Vinci enjoyed there as court painter to Ludovico Sforza, Duke of Milan, was the key that unlocked his genius.

Mr. Syson's contention that Leonardo's great breakthrough came in Milan and not later in Florence, as has generally been accepted until now, has captivated curators, collectors and museum directors who have been generous in loaning works to the show; from the Vatican, Prague, Cracow, Paris and the Royal Collection.

All the pictures on show were painted during da Vinci's 18 years in Milan. Never has it been possible to see so many of da Vinci's paintings together. There are also some 50 drawings, including the monumental "Virgin and Child with Saint Anne and Saint John the Baptist" (sometimes called "The Burlington House Cartoon").

The one picture missing from this period is "The Last Supper", which is painted on a wall. This work, which is badly damaged, is represented here by a large photograph and a near-contemporary (though far inferior) copy. In pages from a notebook da Vinci's slanted "mirror" writing describes the guests at a dinner. With a novelist's interest in detail, he carefully observed the shrug of one man's shoulders, the position of another's hands, the scowl on one face and the frown on yet one more.

The exhibition is arranged thematically; in addition to "Beauty and Love", there is also "Character and Emotion" and "Body and Soul". The visitor quickly comes face to face with the portrait of Ceilia Gallerani, also known as "The Lady with an Ermine".

Although the image is familiar from reproductions, the radiance of the painting is surprising. Further along is an unfinished, yet searing, "Saint Jerome". For the first time, both versions of "The Virgin of the Rocks", one the National Gallery's own and the other belonging to the Louvre, are shown together.

The two versions hang at opposite ends of the long exhibition space. The more one looks at the two pictures, the more visible are the differences between them; the strangely formed rocks in the Louvre's version create a protective atmosphere, whereas in the National Gallery's painting the rocks seem quite eerie, contributing to the overall sepulchral feel of the work.

As a philosopher and scientist, da Vinci strove to understand what he observed in his close studies of nature. Art was an expression of his thoughts. "The Lady with an Ermine" shows the Duke of Milan's teenage mistress in fashionable red gown, its slit sleeves revealing a pale underdress. Da Vinci, always fascinated by knots, carefully details the way the black ribbons are tied on Cecilia's left sleeve. Her right arm is in shadow. The ties on that sleeve are sketchy. The artist has taken into account his observation that visual acuity declines in the dark. The brain fills in necessary information. The sketchiness of the right sleeve helps bring the portait to life, creating what Walter Pater, a 19th-century British essayist and art critic, described as a "reality which almost amounts to illusion".

Da Vinci would sometimes spend years thinking about a single painting. Mr. Syson hopes visitors to the National Gallery will, in turn, look long and hard at these works. Advance tickets for entry to the end of the year had sold out by the opening day. The show does not close until February 5th 2012, but advance tickets for its final weeks are going fast. Meanwhile, the only way to get in now is to queue for one of the 500 tickets being held back for sale each morning. The security checks are elaborate, but the wait is well worth it.

Reading Exercises:

1. How many Leonardo da Vinci's paintings is now preserved?

A. 67

B. 18

C. 9

D. 10

2. The author's main purpose in writing the passage is ______.

A. to introduce the National Gallery

B. to introduce famous paintings and artists in the 15th century

C. to introduce the opportunity to compare Leonardo da Vinci's paintings

D. to introduce Da Vinci's life and his paintings

3. "The Lady with an Ermine" is the other name of the painting?

A. "Character and Emotion".

B. Ceilia Gallerani.

C. "Virgin and Child with Saint Anne and Saint John the Baptist".

D. "Body and Soul".

4. Which of the following statement is Not Correct?

A. Mr. Syson's insists that Leonardo's great breakthrough came in Milan and not later in Florence.

B. The visitor can come face to face with the portrait of Ceilia Gallerani, also known as "The Lady with an Ermine".

C. All the pictures on show were painted during da Vinci's 18 years in Milan.

D. "The Last Supper" will be on the show in the National Gallery.

5. What are we advised to get the tickets to the National Gallery?

A. To buy the advance tickets for entry.

B. To queue for one of the 500 tickets being held back for sale in the morning.

C. To queue for one of the 100 tickets being held back for sale in the morning.

D. To get a free ticket in the National Gallery.

New Words and Phrases

Text A:

sculpt [skʌlpt] *v.* ① to make figures or objects by carving or shaping wood, stone, clay , metal, etc. 雕刻；雕塑 ② to give sth. a particular shape 使具有某种形状

e.g. 1. The figures were sculpted from single blocks of marble.

这些雕像都是用整块大理石雕成的。

e.g. 2. a coastline sculpted by the wind and sea

在风和海水的作用下形成的海岸线

cartography [kɑːˈtɒgrəfi] *n.* the art or process of drawing or making maps 制图学；地图绘制

e.g. Engineering cartography is a subject characteristic of practice.

工程制图是一门实践性很强的技术课。

decipher〔英〕[dɪˈsaɪfə(r)] *v.* to succeed in finding the meaning of sth. that is difficult to read or understand 破译，辨认（难认、难解的东西）

e.g. I'm still no closer to deciphering the code.

我还是无法破译该密码。

contention〔英〕[kənˈtenʃn] *n.* ①angry disagreement between people 争吵；争执；争论 ② a belief or an opinion that you express, especially in an argument（尤指争论时的）看法，观点

e.g. A particular source of contention is plans to privatize state-run companies.

发生争执的一个根源就是国有企业的私有化方案。

breakthrough〔英〕[ˈbreɪkθruː] *v.* an important development that may lead to an agreement or achievement 重大进展；突破

e.g. a major breakthrough in cancer research

癌症研究中的重要突破

monumental〔英〕[ˌmɒnjuˈmentl] *adj.* ① very important and having a great influence, especially as the result of years of work 重要的；意义深远的；不朽的 ② very large, good, bad, stupid, etc. 非常大（或好、坏、蠢等）的

e.g. 1. Gibbon's monumental work "The Rise and Fall of the Roman Empire"

吉本的不朽著作《罗马帝国衰亡史》

e.g. 2. We have a monumental task ahead of us.

极其繁重的工作在等着我们。

shrug〔英〕[ʃrʌg] *v.* to raise your shoulders and then drop them to show that you do not know or care about sth. 耸肩（表示不知道或不在乎）

e.g. The man shrugged his shoulders.

那男子耸了耸肩。

scowl〔英〕[skaʊl] *v.* to look at sb./sth. in an angry or annoyed way 怒视（某人或某物）*n.* an angry look or expression 怒容；不悦的神色

e.g. He scowled, and slammed the door behind him.

他怒气冲冲，摔门而去。

e.g. I wonder why he is wearing an angry scowl.

我不知道他为何面带怒容。

whereas〔英〕[ˌweərˈæz] ① used to compare or contrast two facts（用以比较或对比两个事实）然而，但是，尽管 ② used at the beginning of a sentence in an official document to mean "because of the fact that… "（用于正式文件中句子的开头）鉴于

e.g. Some of the studies show positive results, whereas others do not.

有一些研究结果令人满意，然而其他的则不然。

eerie〔英〕[ˈɪəri] *adj*. strange, mysterious and frightening 怪异的；神秘的；恐怖的

e.g. I found the silence underwater really eerie.

我发觉水下的寂静真令人恐怖。

the more... the more（数量上）越来越多

e.g. She spends more and more time alone in her room.

她一个人待在屋里的时间越来越多。

contribute to 捐献；促成 ; 投稿；有助于

e.g. Heat, cold, tactile and other sensations contribute to flavour.

热、冷、触觉和其他感觉构成了食物风味的一部分。

be fascinated by 被……迷住；被……吸引

e.g. He seems to be fixed and fascinated by the portrait.

他仿佛被那幅肖像迷住了，吸引住了。

take into account 考虑到；顾及

e.g. The company takes account of environmental issues wherever possible.

只要有可能，这家公司总是尽量考虑到环境问题。

decline in 下降

e.g. Government penny-pinching is blamed for the decline in food standards.

政府的吝啬被指责是食品标准下降的原因。

hold back（使）犹豫，踌躇

e.g. She held back, not knowing how to break the terrible news.

她踌躇着，不知如何说出这一可怕的消息。

Text B

Warming-up Activity:

Hawaii is the 50th and most recent state to have joined the United States of America, having received statehood on August 21, 1959. Hawaii is the only U.S. state located in Oceania and the only one composed entirely of islands. It is the northernmost island group in Polynesia, occupying most of an archipelago in the central Pacific Ocean. Hawaii is the only U.S. state located outside North America.

Hawaii

Hawaii is one of the world's best places to visit, and more than six million people visit there each year. Visitors enjoy the beautiful land and the warm weather. It is a paradise that many young couples enjoy during their honeymoon. It is located near the center of the Pacific Ocean, more than six thousand kilometers from Japan. The state of Hawaii is made up of eight main islands. Each island has a wet side and a dry side. It rains much more on the northeast sides of the islands and much more in winter than in summer. This gives each island two different climate areas. One area is dry and desert-like. The other area has green plants, rivers and waterfalls.

When it comes to tourism, Hawaii has something for everyone. The capital and largest city of Hawaii lies about 3900 km from the western coast of the United States. It is a great place for those who wish to experience island life and still keep the conveniences of a large city. White sand beaches offer many activities and views of nearby islands. Hawaii is popular for its greatest sunbathing and good swimming conditions and people can participate in all kinds of water sports. It's one of the sunniest places in the world. A winter day in Hawaii might be called a beautiful day anywhere else. Hawaii has some of the most beautiful, unusual and interesting places on Earth.

Those who wish to experience Hawaii at a slower pace would do well to visit one of the neighboring, less populated islands. All of the neighboring islands offer opportunities to relax and enjoy the sun and scenery. Also, a little over an hour outside of the capital city, on the opposite end of the island you will find a completely different view of Hawaii. Away from the busy city life, the North Shore is known as "the country". You won't find a store on every corner and you won't sit in endless traffic. There is only one hotel, and you will not want to leave!

One moment, you could be relaxing and enjoying the peaceful beauty of the Pacific Ocean, lazily listening to the conversation of your companions. The next moment you could be having your own adventure, seeing the sea life of another world. Hundreds of species of tropical fish can be found in the ocean. It is great fun, seeing lots and lots of fish, coral reefs, and giant sea turtles. What an exciting day it could be, experiencing the ocean and its wonders! Hawaii can make everyone feel like they are part of the natural world.

Some of the most famous attractions of Hawaii are the volcanoes, and you absolutely, positively shouldn't miss them. Hot liquid rock called lava formed the Hawaiian Islands millions of years ago. The lava flowed up from the center of the earth through openings in the sea floor. Visitors today can watch this occur on the Big Island where the world's most active volcano still produces lava everyday. The biggest volcano is over 3000 meters high and is a popular tourist attraction on the island. Many visitors drive to the top of mountain in the morning early hours to watch the sunrise, where, due to its height, it would be better to bring along warm clothes.

Reading Exercises:

Check whether each statement is true (T) or false (F).

1. Hawaii has an abundant rainfall in summer, and its northeast is wetting than other areas.
2. It's a great decision for those who hope to be far from the hectic city to go to Hawaii.
3. The spectacle of Hawaii makes anyone feel like they are part of the natural world.
4. The author believes that visitors could miss the beauty of the volcanoes.
5. The essay talks about Hawaii from the perspective of Tourism.

New Words and Phrases

Text B:

paradise [ˈpærədaɪs] *n.* ① a perfect place where people are said to go when they die（某些宗教所指的）天堂，天国 ② a place that is extremely beautiful and that seems perfect, like heaven 天堂，乐土，乐园（指美好的环境）③ (in the Bible《圣经》) the garden of Eden, where Adam and Eve lived 伊甸园

e.g. 1. The ancient Egyptians saw paradise as an idealized version of their own lives.

古埃及人把天堂视为他们现实生活的理想形式。

e.g. 2. These forests are a hunter's paradise.

这些树林是猎人的乐园。

e.g. 3. Adam and Eve dwelt in paradise.

亚当和夏娃生活在伊甸园里。

honeymoon [ˈhʌnimuːn] *n.* ① a holiday/vacation taken by a couple who have just got married 蜜月 ② the period of time at the start of a new activity when nobody is criticized and people feel enthusiastic（新活动之初的）和谐时期 *v.* to spend your honeymoon somewhere（去某处）度蜜月

e.g. 1. We went to Venice for our honeymoon.

我们去威尼斯度的蜜月。

e.g. 2. The honeymoon period for the government is now over.

这届政府的蜜月期现在已经过去了。

waterfall [ˈwɔːtəfɔːl] *n.* a place where a stream or river falls from a high place, for example over a cliff or rock 瀑布

e.g. Angel Falls, the world's highest waterfall

安赫尔瀑布，世界上最高的瀑布

tourism [ˈtʊərɪzəm] *n.* the business activity connected with providing accommodation, services and entertainment for people who are visiting a place for pleasure 旅游业；观光业

e.g. Tourism is vital for the Spanish economy.

旅游业对西班牙经济至关重要。

convenience [kənˈviːniəns] *n.* ① the quality of being useful, easy or suitable for sb. 方便；适宜；便利 ② something that is useful and can make things easier or quicker to do, or more comfortable 便利的事物（或设施）；方便的用具

e.g. 1. We have provided seats for the convenience of our customers.

为方便顾客我们备有座位。

e.g. 2. Some TVRs have power steering and conveniences such as central locking and powered windows.

一些特雷沃车型配有动力转向系统以及中央锁和电动窗之类的便利装置。

sunbathe [ˈsʌnbeɪð] *v.* to sit or lie in the sun, especially in order to go brown (get a suntan) 沐日光浴；晒太阳

e.g. Franklin swam and sunbathed at the pool every morning.

每天上午富兰克林都在游泳池中游泳，在池边晒太阳。

companion [kəmˈpæniən] *n.* ① a person or an animal that travels with you or spends a lot of time with you 旅伴；伴侣；陪伴 ② a person who shares in your work, pleasures, sadness, etc. 同甘共苦的伙伴

e.g. 1. Fred had been her constant companion for the last six years of her life.

在她生命的最后 6 年，弗莱德一直是她忠实的伴侣。

e.g. 2. We became companions in misfortune.

我们成了患难之交。

四级真题中的使用：

“Energy independence” and its rhetorical（修辞的）companion “energy security” are, however, slippery concepts that are rarely thought through.

volcano [vɒlˈkeɪnəʊ] *n.* a mountain with a large opening at the top through which gases and lava (= hot liquid rock) are forced out into the air, or have been in the past

火山

e.g. An active volcano may erupt at any time.

活火山会随时喷发。

lava [ˈlɑːvə] *n.* Lava is the very hot liquid rock that comes out of a volcano.（火山）熔岩

e.g. The lava will just ooze gently out of the crater.

岩浆就会从火山口缓缓涌流出来。

make up of 构成；组成

e.g. Men make up 56% of the student numbers.

男生占学生总数的 56%。

participate in 分担；参加；参与；插脚；插足

e.g. Over half the population of this country participate in sport.

这个国家一半以上的人口参加体育锻炼。

flow up 向上涌动

e.g. As the plates separate, hot molten mantle material flows up to fill the void.

随着板块的分开，炽热的熔融地幔物质向上流动，以填充空隙。

drive to 开车去

e.g. Atlanta was only an hour's drive to the north.

开车往北仅 1 个小时就能到达亚特兰大。

due to 由于；因为

e.g. It was a real prize due to its rarity and good condition.

因为稀有并且品相完好，它价值连城。

Writing

Part 1 命题分析

应用文类 A

图表作文

1. 定义

图表作文是通过提供的一组或几组数据来反映某种趋势或某一问题、现象。要求考生对图表中的相关数据进行描述、分析和评论，并得出合乎逻辑的结论。它是将数据、形象信息转换为文字信息的过程。图表作文要求的不是对图表的简单叙述，而是抓住图表所反映的主要问题。因为图表式作文所要讨论的现象和问题都隐含在数据里，所以考生常会觉得此类作文比较难写。要想抓住主旨，就要分析图表中那些最有代表性、规律性的数字，或变化大的数字。

2. 写作步骤

图表式作文写作分三步：

第一步：开门见山地点明本图表所反映的主题

常使用的词汇有 table、chart、figure、graph、describe、tell、show、represent 等。

常用句型：

（1）The graph/chart/table above shows...

（2）From the above graph/chart, it can be seen that...

（3）As is shown in the graph, ...

（4）The chart/table shows the differences between…

第二步：分析数据间的主要差异及趋势，然后描写（在描写数据间变化及总趋势特征时，可采用分类式或对比式以支持主题，并阐明必要的理由）。注意层次。

常用的转折、对比及比较词汇：while、but、on the contrary、however、compare with、in contrast to、as…as、the same as、be similar to、be different between、among、more than、less than。

常用描写趋势变化的词汇：increase、rise、go up、reduce、drop、go down、fall、reach、remain、by/to、slowly、slightly、gradually、sharply、rapidly、the number of…、from…to 及比较级、倍数等。

常用句型：

Facts:

(1) There was a great /slight increase /rise in….

(2) There has been a sudden/slow/rapid fall/drop in….

(3) It is 20% lower/higher than….

(4) The number /rate has nearly doubled, as against that of last year.

(5) The number is …times as much as that of….

(6) It increases/rises/decreases/reduces by…/…% / two thirds.

(7) By comparison with…, it decreased/increased/fell from…to….

Reasons:

(1) The reason for…is that….

(2) One may think of the change as a result of….

(3) The change in…largely results from the fact that….

(4) There are several causes for this significant growth in….First,…. Second,….

(5) This brings out the important fact that….

第三步：归纳总结或发表评论（展望未来或提出方法或建议）。

常用词汇：

(1) in a word / in short /generally speaking

(2) It's clear from the chart that….

(3) In summary, it is important….

(4) From what has been discussed above, we can draw the conclusion that….

(5) Obviously, if we want to…, it is necessary….

(6) There is no doubt that attention must be paid….

需注意以下几点：

（1）图表上的内容 / 数据无须全部描述；

（2）善于抓总的规律、趋势，归纳增减率；

（3）描述时应注意动词时态。叙述特定时间的情况应用一般过去时，叙述经常出现的情况或自己的评述则用一般现在时。

Part 2 练习

Directions: *For this part, you are allowed 30 minutes to write a composition on the topic **Traveling Abroad**. You should write at least 120 words according to the outline given below in Chinese*:

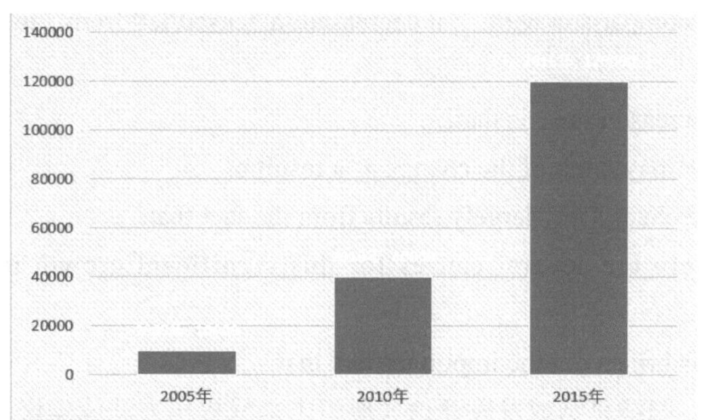

（1）近十年来X市有越来越多的人选择出境旅游；

（2）出现这种现象的原因；

（3）这种现象可能产生的影响。

【审题】本题属于提纲式图表命题。提纲第一点要求指出一种现象，提纲第二点要求分析这种现象产生的原因，提纲第三点要求阐述这种现象可能产生的影响，由此可判断本文应为现象解释类作文。

【中心思想】根据所给提纲，本文应包含以下内容：简要描述图表中所反映的近十年来X市选择出境旅游的人数情况，以及旅游人数的变化情况；分析导致这一变化的主要原因；说明该现象可能带来的影响。

【范文】

Traveling Abroad

From the chart, we clearly learn that there has been a sharp rise in the number of people traveling abroad in X city in the past decade. As early as in 1995, the number of people traveling abroad was only about 10,000. Then only 5 years later, it increased to nearly 40,000.And by 2015, the number had reached over 120,000, which was twelve times what it was ten years ago.

There are many reasons accounting for this change.Firstly, it is due to the increase of people's incomes in X city. People are better off many times than China' s Deepening reform and opening up has been in effect for many years, which create more chances for people to travel abroad. Finally, the development of travel industry leads to the increase, which provides people with a good opportunity to have a better understanding of the culture, history and customs in foreign countries.

As far as I am concerned, the increasing number of people traveling abroad might have both its advantages and disadvantages. For one thing, it enhances economic and cultural communication among X city and other cities in the world. For another, the improper behavior of some tourists may damage the image of our country. To conclude, it is necessary for each tourist to behave himself/herself well wherever he/she travels in the world. Our Chinese tourists to pay more attention to our behaviors when we travel abroad.（说明影响段）

Vocabulary Exercise

A. *Fill in the blanks with the words in the box. Read the sentences carefully before making your choices. You may not use any of the words in the bank more than once. Change the form where necessary.*

shrug volcano breakthrough whereas decipher waterfall lava companion sculpt honeymoon monumental scowl eerie contention tourism cartography sunbathe paradise convenience

1. These ________ tools have evolved through their use, and each one has a different form which matches its function.
2. J.H. Lambert initiated a new epoch in the theoretical ________ .
3. It is a headache to ________ his sloppy penmanship.
4. Sufficient research evidence exists to support this ________ .
5. He finally has a ________ in his creation.
6. When the verdict was announced a year ago, the 2-year jail sentence for Dr. Fadl was hailed as a ________ victory by campaigners.
7. They would ________ their shoulders, and treat you like a child.
8. The boss manifested his disgust with a ________.
9. His children are well bred, ________ those of his sister's are naughty.
10. The sky had an ________ yellow-orange hue, with the sun glowing behind a peculiar haze.
11. Hawaii's fruit flies are the birds of ________ of the insect world.

12. They flew to the West Indies on _________.

13. We have nice places like beaches, _________ , cities like St. Paulo and good people.

14. _________ in Egypt has been the country's major source of cash.

15. Infrastructures will also be improved to provide more _________ for the tourists.

16. Sometimes we go to the beach and at other times we _________ on the patio.

17. The dog is a loyal _________ . He makes us feel safe.

18. The erupting _________ was an awe-inspiring sight.

19. The _________ now moving at a pace of 150 yards a day.

B. *Fill in the blanks with the phrases in the box. Read the sentences carefully before making your choices. You may not use any of the phrases in the bank more than once. Change the form where necessary.*

drive to	contribute to	be fascinated by	take into account	due to	holding...back
the more...the more	flow up	made up of	participate in	decline in	

1. _________ complex the problem, _________ the need for simplicity.

2. Honesty and hard work _________ success and happiness.

3. Take a boat trip, and you will _________ the peaks along the river.

4. Coursework is _________ as well as exam results.

5. Unemployment has led to a 30% _________ income-tax revenues since 2002.

6. The police were convinced the man was _________ something _________.

7. Society is _________ a variety of people; some are good, others (are) bad, and still others (are) in between.

8. They expected him to _________ the ceremony.

9. Twin Disc Check Valves can be installed horizontally or in the vertical position with _________ .

10. How long does it take him to _________ work?

11. Great changes are in prospect in this area _________ foreign investment.

Extended Exercises

Cloze

There is a passage with 10 blanks. You are required to select one word for each blank from a list of choices in a word bank following the passage. Read the passage through carefully before making your choices. Each choice in the bank is identified by a letter.

A) abnormal	B) applied	C) briefly	D) categorizing
E) challenges	F) figure	G) percentage	H) proving
I) regardless	J) searched	K) similarities	L) slightly
M) suggests	N) tastes	O) traditional	

Many men and women have long bought into the idea that there are "male" and "female" brains, believing that explains just about every difference between the sexes. A new study __1__ that belief, questioning whether brains really can be distinguished by gender.

In the study, Tel Aviv University researchers __2__ for sex differences the entire human brain.

And what did they find? Not much. Rather than offer evidence for __3__ brains as "male" or "female" research shows that brains fall into a wide range, with most people falling right in the middle.

Daphna Joel, who led the study, said her research found that while there are some gender-based __4__, many different types of brain can't always be distinguished by gender.

While the "average" male and "average" female brains were __5__ different, you couldn't tell it by looking at individual brain scans. Only a small __6__ of people had "all-male" or "all-female" characteristics.

Larry Cahill, an American neuroscientist（神经科学家）, said the study is an important addition to a growing body of research questioning __7__ beliefs about gender and brain function. But he cautioned against concluding from this study that all brains are the same, __8__ of gender.

"There's a mountain of evidence __9__ the importance of sex influences at all levels of brain function," he told The Seattle Times.

If anything, he said, the study ___10___ that gender plays a very important role in the brain "even when we are not clear exactly how".

Paragraph Matching

You are going to read a passage with ten statements attached to it. Each statement contains information given in one of the paragraphs. Identify the paragraph from which the information is derived. You may choose a paragraph more than once. Each paragraph is marked with a letter.

Can Burglars Jam Your Wireless Security System?

[A] Any product that promises to protect your home deserves careful examination. So it isn't surprising that you'll find plenty of strong opinions about the potential vulnerabilities of popular home-security systems.

[B] The most likely type of burglary（入室盗窃）by far is the unsophisticated crime of opportunity, usually involving a broken window or some forced entry. According to the FBI, crimes like these accounted roughly two-thirds of all household burglaries in the US in 2013. The wide majority of the rest were illegal, unforced entries that resulted from something like a window being left open. The odds of a criminal using technical means to bypass a security system are so small that the FBI doesn't even track those statistics.

[C] One of the main theoretical home-security concerns is whether or not a given system is vulnerable to being blocked from working altogether. With wired setups, the fear is that a burglar（入室盗贼）might be able to shut your system down simply by cutting the right cable. With a wireless setup, you stick battery-powered sensors up around your home that keep an eye on windows, doors, motion, and more. If they detect something wrong while the system is armed, they'll transmit a wireless alert signal to a base station that will then raise the alarm. That approach will eliminate most cord-cutting concerns—but what about their wireless equivalent, jamming? With the right device tuned to the right frequency, what's to stop a thief from jamming your setup and blocking that alert signal from ever reaching the base station?

[D] Jamming concerns are nothing new, and they're not unique to security systems. Any device that's built to receive a wireless signal at a specific frequency can be overwhelmed by a stronger signal coming in on the same frequency. For comparison, let's say you wanted to "jam" a conversation between two people—all you'd need to do is yell in the listener's ear.

[E] Security devices are required to list the frequencies they broadcast on—that means that a potential thief can find what they need to know with minimal Googling. They will, however, need to know what system they're looking for. If you have a sign in your yard declaring what setup you use, that'd point them in the right direction, though at that point, we're talking about a highly targeted, semi-sophisticated attack, and not the sort forced-entry attack that makes up the majority of burglaries. It's easier to find and acquire jamming equipment for some frequencies than it is for others.

[F] Wireless security providers will often take steps to help combat the threat of jamming attacks. SimpliSafe, winner of our Editor's Choice distinction, utilizes a special system that's capable of separating incidental RF interference from targeted jamming attacks. When the system thinks it's being jammed, it'll notify you via push alert（推送警报）. From there, it's up to you to sound the alarm manually.

[G] SimpliSafe was singled out in one recent article on jamming, complete with a video showing the entire system being effectively bypassed with handheld jamming equipment. After taking appropriate measures to contain the RF interference to our test lab, we tested the attack out for ourselves, and were able to verify that it's possible with the right equipment. However, we also verified that SimpliSafe's anti-jamming system works. It caught us in the act, sent an alert to my smartphone, and also listed our RF interference on the system's event log. The team behind the article and video in question made no mention of the system, or whether or not it detected them.

[H] We like the unique nature of that software. It means that a thief likely wouldn't be able to Google how the system works, then figure out a way around it.

Even if they could, SimpliSafe claims that its system is always evolving, and that it varies slightly from system to system, which means there wouldn't be a universal magic formula for cracking it. Other systems also seem confident on the subject of jamming. The team at Frontpoint addresses the issue in a blog on its site, citing their own jam protection software and claiming that there aren't any documented cases of successful jam attack since the company began offering wireless security sensors in the 1980s.

[I] Jamming attacks are absolutely possible. As said before, with the right equipment and the right know-how, it's possible to jam any wireless transmission. But how probable is it that someone will successfully jam their way into your home and steal your stuff?

[J] Let's imagine that you live in a small home with a wireless security setup that offers a functional anti-jamming system. First, a thief is going to need to target your home, specifically. Then, he's going to need to know the technical details of your system and acquire the specific equipment necessary for jamming your specific setup. Presumably, you keep your doors locked at night and while you're away. So the thief will still need to break in. That means defeating the lock somehow, or breaking a window. He'll need to be jamming you at this point, as a broken window or opened door would normally release the alarm. So, too, would the motion detectors in your home, so the thief will need to continue jamming once he's inside and searching for things to steal. However, he'll need to do so without tripping the anti-jamming system, the details of which he almost certainly does now have access to.

[K] At the end of the day, these kinds of systems are primarily designed to protect against the sort of opportunistic smash-and-grab attack that makes up the majority of burglaries. They're also only a single layer in what should ideally be a many-sided approach to securing your home, one that includes common sense things like sound locks and proper exterior lighting at night. No system is impenetrable, and none can promise to eliminate the worst case completely. Every one of them has vulnerabilities that a knowledgeable thief could theoretically exploit. A good system is one that keeps that worst-case setting as improbable as possible while also offering strong protection in the event of a less-extraordinary attack.

1. It is possible for burglars to make jamming attacks with the necessary equipment and skill.
2. Interfering with a wireless security system is similar to interfering with a conversation.
3. A burglar has to continuously jam the wireless security device to avoid triggering the alarm, both inside and outside the house.
4. SimpliSafe provides devices that are able to distinguish incidental radio interference from targeted jamming attacks.
5. Only a very small proportion of burglaries are committed by technical means.
6. It is difficult to crack SimpliSafe as its system keeps changing.
7. Wireless devices will transmit signals so as to activate the alarm once something wrong is detected.
8. Different measures should be taken to protect one's home from burglary in addition to the wireless security system.
9. SimpliSafe's device can send a warning to the house owner's cellphone.
10. Burglars can easily get a security device's frequency by Internet search.

Cultural Translation

Directions: *For this part, you are allowed 30 minutes to translate a passage from Chinese into English. You should write your answer on Answer Sheet 2.*

在中国文化中，红色通常象征着好运、长寿和幸福，在春节和其他喜庆场合，红色到处可见。人们把现金作为礼物送给家人或亲密朋友时，通常放在红信封里。红色在中国流行的另一个原因是人们把它与中国革命和共产党相联系。然而，红色并不总是代表好运与快乐。因为从前死者的名字常用红色书写，用红墨水写中国人名被看成一种冒犯行为。

练习答案

Reading Exercises

Text A: 1 ～ 5 BCBDB

Text B: 1 ～ 5 TTFFT

Vocabulary Exercises

A:

1. sculpting
2. cartography
3. decipher
4. contention
5. breakthrough
6. monumental
7. shrug
8. scowl
9. whereas
10. eerie
11. paradise
12. honeymoon
13. waterfall
14. Tourism
15. convenience
16. sunbathe
17. companion
18. volcano
19. lava

B:

1. The more...the more
2. contribute to
3. be fascinated by

4. taken into account
5. decline in
6. holding...back
7. made up of
8. participate in
9. flow up
10. drive to
11. due to

Extended Exercises

Cloze:

1 ~ 10: EJDKL GOIHM

Paragraph Matching:

1 ~ 10: IDJFB HCKGE

Cultural Translation:

The color of red in Chinese culture usually means good luck, longevity and happiness. Red can be found everywhere during Chinese Spring Festival and other joyous occasions. Cash often sent to family members or close friends as a gift is in a red envelope. The other reason why red is so popular in China is that people worship red and connect it with Chinese revolution and the communist party. However, it does not always equal to good luck and joy in that the name of the dead used to be written in red. Using red ink to write names of Chinese people was seen as an offense.

Unit 4 Mysteries of the Universe

Learning Objectives

After completing this unit, you will be able to do the following:

◇ Practice for the skill: How to identify the types of questions;

◇ Grasp the main idea and the structure of the texts;

◇ Master the key languagc points and grammatical structure in the text;

◇ Conduct a series of reading, speaking and writing activities related to the theme in the unit.

Learning Difficult Points

In this unit, you will learn some difficult points listed below.

◇ Listening: How to identify the types of questions.

◇ Writing: Applied Writing

Outline

The Following are the main sections in this Unit.

1. Listening
2. Speaking
3. Reading: Text A & Text B
4. Writing
5. Extended Exercises

Vocabulary

Listed below are some words appearing in this unit that you should make part of your vocabulary.

dwarf
solar system
spacecraft
astronomer
gravitational
capture
telescope
miscalculation
on the edge of
shed (new) light on
turn into
pick out
turn out

Looking Ahead

Mysteries of the Universe

Science can not solve the ultimate mystery of nature. And that is because, in the last analysis, we ourselves are a part of the mystery that we are trying to solve.

—Max Planck

Introduction

Stephen Hawking is a world-renowned British theoretical physicist, known for his contributions to the fields of cosmology, general relativity and quantum gravity, especially in the context of black holes.

In the 1980s, he began to question the Big Bang theory itself, suggesting that perhaps there never was a start and would be no end, but just change, a constant transition of one "universe" giving way to another through glitches in space-time. He developed his "No Boundary Proposal" in collaboration with the American physicist Jim Hartle. Under classical general relativity, the universe either has to be infinitely old or has started at a singularity, but Hawking and Hartle's proposal raises a third possibility: that the universe is finite but had no initial singularity to produce a boundary. The history of his no-boundary universe in "imaginary time" can be best envisaged using the analogy of the surface of the Earth's North Pole.

Speaking

Consider the following questions before reading:

1. What is a mystery? Can you define it?
2. What are the mysteries in the universe?

Conversation

Study and practice the conversation below.

A: There are so many stars in the sky. Oh, so beautiful! Do you think there are aliens on other planets?

B: Maybe. I've been curious about that since I was a little girl.

A: Me, too. And I do want to know the origin of the universe.

B: Scientists are doing experiments along the Swiss-French border to find the secrets of the universe.

A: But it is reported that the LHC has been damaged again.

B: Why?

A: Because there's a little piece of bread in the LHC. Scientists believe it was left by a bird.

B: That's impossible. The LHC lies in an underground tunnel.

A: Well, they claimed that a bird from the future left the bread.

B: Oh, I just can't believe it.

UNIT 4 Mysteries of the Universe

Listening

Listening skills are fundamental to success in ENGLISH Listening. Through this part, we will have a detailed introduction to promote listening efficiency we could enhance by analyzing the three parts—News, Long conversation and Passage.

Listening Skills for Long Conversation (2)

Keys to identify the types of questions

Three types of questions are common in long conversations.

The first type is to test students' ability to gain the main idea of the conversation, to be clear of the relationship of the two speakers, and to get the place where the conversation is taking place. e.g. What are the speakers mainly talking about? What is the man's purpose in calling the woman? What is the man's chief complaint? Where is the woman at the time of the conversation?

The second type is designed to test students' comprehension of some important details-to know what happens exactly, the cause and effect, the character of the people. e.g. What did the woman advise the man to do? What caused the incident?

The third type is to test students' comprehension in analyzing, inferring, or making certain summary. e.g. What do we learn about the man from the conversation? e.g. How does the woman interpret the fact that the man was asked to help his colleagues with their work? e.g. Why does the man prefer to cook a meal rather than have a take-away? What does the man say about an element of stress in his job? What does the woman think of the police fining drivers?

Example（出自四级听力原文）

W: This is Kerry Burke from *New York Daily News*. I'm speaking to Delroy Simmonds, an unemployed Brooklyn man who missed a job interview Tuesday for the best of reasons: He was saving the life of a 9-month-old boy who was blown into the path of an oncoming subway train by a high wind.

女：我是《纽约每日新闻》的记者 Kerry Burke。我正在采访 Delroy Simmonds，布鲁克林的一位失业男士，他周二因为一个极佳的理由错过了一场面试：他当时正在救一个因为大风被吹到铁路上的 9 个月大的男婴，当时正有火车驶来。

M: Everybody is making me out to be some sort of superhero. I'm just an ordinary person, and a father of two. Anybody in that situation would have done what I did.

男：大家都在说我是超级英雄。我只是一个普通的人，两个孩子的父亲。任何人在我当时的处境下都会那么做的。

W: You were going to an interview when the

incident occurred, right?

女：事情发生的时候，您正要去一个面试，对吧？

M: Yes, I was on my way to apply for a maintenance position. I've been looking for a job for a year and more. I'm looking for something to support my family.

男：是的，我正要去竞聘一个维修师的职位。我已经找工作找了一年多了。我正在找点儿事情做，养家糊口。

W: Tell us what happened at the station.

女：给我们讲讲当时在车站的情形吧。

M: There was a strong wind. It had to be 30 to 40 miles an hour. There was a woman with four kids. One was in a pushchair. The wind blew the baby onto the tracks.

男：当时刮着很大的风，得有时速 30 ～ 40 英里。有一位女士带着 4 个孩子。其中一个还在推车里。大风把孩子刮到了铁路上。

W: Witnesses said people were looking on in horror as the child's mother, identified by sources as Maria Zamara, stood frozen in shock. In the distance, people could see the train rounding a bend, headed into the station. I guess you were not aware of any of these, right?

女：目击者称周围的人都一脸惊恐，而孩子的母亲 Maria Zamara 当时都被吓傻了。不远处，火车就在拐角的地方驶入站台。我猜您当时压根儿没注意到这些事情吧？

M: No. I just jumped down and grabbed the

Questions12,13 are the third type questions, to test students' ability in making summary and reference.

Questions14, 15 are the second type questions, to test students' comprehension in details e.g. cause and effect.

baby. The train was coming around the corner as I lifted the baby from the tracks. I really wasn't thinking.

男：没有。我跳下去，抓住孩子。我把孩子抓起来的时候火车正在拐弯。我当时真没多想。

W: What an amazing story. Thank you very much.

女：真是个惊人的故事。非常感谢您。

Questions 12 to 15 are based on the conversation you have just heard.

请根据你刚刚听到的对话回答问题 12 至问题 15。

Question 12. What did Kerry Burke from *New York Daily News* say about the man?

问题 12.《纽约每日新闻》记者 Kerry Burke 怎么评价那位男士？

Question 13. What do we learn about the man from the conversation?

问题 13. 从对话中我们能知道有关那位男士的什么信息？

Question 14. What caused the incident?

问题 14. 是什么造成了这次事故？

Question 15. How did the mother react when the incident occurred?

问题 15. 事故发生的时候，那位母亲什么反应？

Reading

Text A

Warming-up Activity:

The Solar System is the gravitationally bound system comprising the Sun and the objects that orbit it, either directly or indirectly. It formed 4. 6 billion years ago from the gravitational collapse of a giant interstellar molecular cloud. The four smaller inner planets, Mercury, Venus, Earth and Mars, are terrestrial planets. The four outer planets are giant planets, being substantially more massive than the terrestrials. The two largest, Jupiter and Saturn, are gas giants while the two outermost planets, Uranus and Neptune, are ice giants. All eight planets have almost circular orbits that lie within a nearly flat disc called the ecliptic.

Pluto

Pluto sits on the edge of our solar system, three and a half billion miles from earth. Remote but not forgotten. For generations of school children, Pluto is the ninth planet. But on Aug 24th, 2006, Pluto lost its planetary status.

It was reclassified as a dwarf planet. "Pluto doesn't care what we call it, it doesn't care what we call it. It's gonna be the same object whether we call it planet or dwarf planet or minor planet." "Pluto has all the characteristics of the other planets, in the same way that Chihuahua is a dog, just smaller. Dwarf planets are planets, there's small variety."

Pluto sits on an exiting new frontier of space exploration. A state of the art base craft is heading towards it at around a million miles a day. Scientists hope that it will shed new light on the formation of the solar system and even the birth of our own planet. "Every time we take a spacecraft and go by a new body, it turns into an entire world that is filled with fascinating phenomena that we would have never understood before." "The fact that Pluto is so far away, is so small, so dim, and may represent now a whole new swath of real estate worth of object, tells us that Pluto has a lot in store for us to learn about it."

Our story starts with Pluto's discovery. By the early 20th century, 8 planets have been discovered. Many assume that Neptune is the outermost, but astronomer Percival Lowell is convinced that there is another planet out there—a massive planet whose gravitational pull is disturbing Neptune's orbit. He calls it Planet X, but it proves elusive and for good reason: the giant planet theory is wrong. "The original motivations for searching for Pluto were based on bad data basically. They just didn't have enough information then and good enough data to really solve this problem."

By 1929, astronomers at Lowell's observatory outside Flagstaff, Arizona, have been searching for planet X for 14 fruitless years. 23-year-old amateur astronomer Clyde Tombaugh joins the team and is given the painstaking task of comparing vast numbers of star-like objects. Tombaugh captures the images onto large photographic plates, using a 12 inch telescope, small by today's standard. He is looking for tiny points of light that have moved across the night sky. Stars remain fixed while planets moved. Tombaugh continued the search for over a year. Then examining the plates taken on 23rd, 29th of January, 1930—a faint object catches his eye.

Flicking between these two images, he sees that the object appears to have moved. He checks and rechecks, making sure it isn't a comet or a blemish on the plate. It seems the young astronomer has discovered the astronomical Holy Grail: Planet X.

"He also was extremely lucky to be looking at the right part of the sky at the right time and of course, he was, had very keen eyes and skillfully able to pick out that small object as it moved across the sky." Even though the giant planet theory turned out to be wrong, Tombaugh still found the planet.

The new discovery is headline news. The planet is named Pluto after the Greek God of the underworld. Based on their original miscalculation, they believe Pluto is bigger than earth. Pluto officially becomes the solar system's ninth planet.

The results are surprising, Pluto is not larger than earth, in fact it's smaller than our own moon. Side by side, Pluto and Charon only cover the width of the United States.

Mars

In December 1903 Orville and Wilbur Wright's Flyer lifted off the ground for the first time, near Kitty Hawk, North Carolina, and proved that powered, controlled flight was possible on Earth. On April 19th, at 7 : 34 am Universal Time, a small American helicopter called *Ingenuity* proved it works on another world, too. Following an intricately planned flight sequence six years in the making, the 1. 8kg craft spun its contra-rotating twin rotor-blades at 2400 rpm, to ascend from the surface of Mars. It climbed to an altitude of three metres, hovered for 30 seconds, took a photograph of its own shadow (pictured) and touched back down on the ground.

Flying conditions on Mars are rather different from those on Earth. Though it has only a third of Earth's gravity at its surface, which sounds as if it might make the task of flying there easier, Mars's atmosphere has a mere hundredth of the density of Earth's. This means there is little air to push against when attempting to fly. To compensate, *Ingenuity*'s blades spin five times faster than those of a typical helicopter on Earth.

To keep its flight stable with such fast-moving blades requires hundreds of adjustments a second, based on a stream of information from sensors aboard the aircraft. This complexity explains why the test flight, which was supposed to happen a week ago, was delayed. The project's engineers identified software problems during a high-speed spin-test of the rotors, and these had to be fixed.

Ingenuity's flight brings space scientists closer to a new way of exploring other worlds. Over several decades, rovers designed by NASA, America's space agency, have become ever-more sophisticated mobile laboratories. But they still moves lowly and cautiously, and can operate only over reasonably flat ground. Future flying machines could carry payloads around quickly, or survey wide areas of terrain, regardless of its roughness. They could also fly close up to cliff faces that have interesting-looking rock formations, or deep into cave systems.

Despite the daunting engineering challenges required, NASA already has plans to use such machines in future exploration. In 2026 a mission called *Dragonfly* will, if all goes well, be launched towards Titan, a moon of Saturn. Using eight rotors, this aircraft will carry its suite of scientific instruments to dozens of places, to examine the habitability of the local environment and perhaps look for signs of life.

Ingenuity does not carry any instruments, since it is just a technology demonstrator, though it will send back pictures of its travels. Despite its diminutive size and capabilities, however, the aircraft has now been given the official designation "IGY" by the International Civil Aviation Organisation — the United Nations agency responsible for such matters. In homage to the builders of *Flyer*, it also carries a small piece of cloth from one of *Flyer*'s wings, and its Martian aerodrome will henceforth be known as Wright Brothers Field.

Reading Exercises:

1. What is the main idea in *Pluto*?

A. The time when Pluto was discovered.

B. The place where Pluto was discovered.

C. The reason why Pluto needs to be discovered.

D. How Pluto was discovered.

2. Dr. Alan Stern compare Pluto with a Chihuahua for the reason?

A. They look like almost the same.

B. Both of them are little known stars.

C. They are both smaller but has all the features of their type.

D. They are both well-known stars.

3. Which of the following statement is Correct according to the text ?

A. Pluto is on the edge of our solar system, three and a half million miles from the earth.

B. Pluto is usually called dwarf planet or minor planet.

C. Pluto does not have the features of other planets.

D. Neptune is the remotest planet from the sun in the solar system.

4. Why is the planet got the name "Pluto"?

A. It is named after the person who discovered it.

B. It is named after the Greek God of underworld.

C. It is named according to its order in the solar system.

D. It is named according to the place where it was found.

5. What is the size of Pluto mentioned by Dr. Mark Buie?

A.Larger than the earth.

B.The same size as the moon.

C.The same size as the earth.

D.Smaller than the moon.

New Words and Phrases

Text A:

dwarf [dwɔ:f] *n.*an extremely small person, who will never grow to a normal size because of a physical problem 矮子；侏儒

e.g. The dwarf 's long arms were not proportional to his height.

那侏儒的长臂与他的身高不成比例。

Neptune [ˈneptju:n] *n.* a giant planet with a ring of ice particles; the 8th planet from the sun 海王星

e.g. Neptune turned out to be a dynamic, stormy world.

海王星原来是个有生气、多风暴的世界。

spacecraft [ˈspeɪskrɑ:ft] *n.* a rocket or other vehicle that can travel in space 宇宙飞船；航天器

e.g. The spacecraft made a successful reentry into the earth's atmosphere.

宇宙飞船成功地重返大气层。

astronomer [əˈstrɒnəmə(r)] *n.* a scientist who studies the stars, planets, and other natural objects in space 天文学家

e.g. A prominet Soviet astronomer puts it well.

一位著名的苏联天文学家对此有过十分精辟的描绘。

gravitational [ˌgrævɪˈteɪʃənl] *adj.* relating to or resulting from the force of gravity 万有引力的

e.g. If a spacecraft travels faster than 11 km a second, it escapes the earth's gravitational pull.

如果飞行速度超过每秒 11 千米，宇宙飞船将摆脱地球的引力。

capture [ˈkæptʃə(r)] *v.* ① to catch a person or an animal and keep them as a prisoner or in a confined space 俘虏 ② to make sb. interested in sth. 引起（注意、想象、兴趣）

e.g. The whole town celebrated when two tanks were captured.

全城居民庆祝缴获了两辆坦克。

四级真题中的使用：

1. Steamships captured the North Atlantic passenger business from sail in the 1840s because of its much greater speed.
2. Some businesses will benefit but the vast bulk of the savings will be captured by workers, not their employers.
3. Humanity also has been obsessed with trying to capture the meaning of time.

telescope [ˈtelɪskəʊp] *n.* a long instrument shaped like a tube. It has lenses inside it that make distant things seem larger and nearer when you look through it. 望远镜

e.g. It's hoped that the telescope will enable scientists to see deeper into the universe than ever before.

人们希望望远镜能使科学家看到比以往更遥远的宇宙深处。

miscalculation [ˌmɪskælkjʊ'leɪʃn] *v.* make a mistake in judging a situation or in making a calculation. 误算

e.g. It's clear that he has badly miscalculated the mood of the people...

显然，他完全没有想到人们的情绪会是如此。

四级真题中的使用：

Kodak's decision not to pursue the role of official film for the 1984 Los Angeles Olympics was a major miscalculation.

on the edge of 濒于；几乎；在边缘

e.g. She was perched on the edge of the sofa.

她坐在沙发沿上。

shed (new) light on 为……提供线索；对……透露情况；使……清楚地显出；阐明……

e.g. These Clausewitzian commonplaces will shed light on the grotesque fiasco at Leyte Gulf.

Clausewtzian 这几句平易浅显的话，可以说明莱特湾那一次近似荒唐的失败原因。

turn into（使）变成；译成；成为

e.g. We think he'll turn into a top-class player.

我们认为他会成为一流的选手。

pick out 挑选；取出；了解；衬托

e.g. We must pick out the enemy's weakest units for attack.

我们必须找敌人最薄弱的部位攻击。

turn out 结果是；关掉；制造；出席

e.g. Our photograph shows how the plants will turn out.

我们的照片展示了植物的生长状况。

solar system 太阳系

e.g. Saturn is the second biggest planet in the solar system.

土星是太阳系中的第二大行星。

Text B

Warming-up Activity:

Mermaids may not exist, but the ocean is still full of mysteries.

Those large, beautiful bodies of water are home to an infinite number of strange creatures and bewildering phenomena. The average ocean depth is 14,000 feet deep-that leaves a lot of room for the mysterious, the mythical and everything in between.

Humpback Whale Facts

Humpback whale, is a baleen whale known for its elaborate courtship songs and displays. Humpbacks usually range from 12 to 16 metres (39 to 52 feet) in length and weigh approximately 36 metric tons. The body is black on the upper surface, with a variable amount of white below, and it has about 30 broad ventral grooves on the throat and chest. This cetacean is distinguished from other baleen whales by its long, narrow flippers, which are about a third as long as the body and scalloped on the forward edge. Humpbacks also have large knobs on the head, jaws, and body, each knob being associated with one or two hairs. The dorsal fin is small and set far back on the body.

Humpback whales live along the coasts of all oceans, occasionally swimming close to shore, even into harbours and rivers. They undertake long migrations between polar feeding grounds in summer and tropical or subtropical breeding grounds in winter. Diet consists of shrimp like crustaceans called krill, small fish, and plankton, which the humpback whale strains out of the water with its baleen. Humpbacks use a unique method of feeding called bubblenetting, in which bubbles are exhaled as the whale swims in a spiral below a patch of water dense with food. The curtain of bubbles confines the prey to a small area in the middle of which one or more whales surface.

Every humpback can be identified from the unique marking on the underside of its tail. They can dive for up to 45 minutes and can reach depths of 600 feet. Humpbacks can weigh two tons at birth. A full-grown whale can be 45 feet long and weigh up to 40 tons. Nearly 40 percent of a humpback's body weight is muscle. They can see up to 400 feet underwater. They can blow out air from their blowholes at a speed of 300 mph . Their lungs can hold 2,500 gallons of air.

When Lady Gaga releases a new single, it quickly goes around the world. Now scientists have discovered the same thing happens with the songs of another unusual and interesting creature-the humpback whale. The mammals become interested in new tunes just like people do, and the most popular original whale songs spread globally like hit singles. The discovery has astonished experts who say it is the first time such a large, "population-wide cultural exchange" has been seen in the animal kingdom.

Male humpback whales are well-known for the loud, long and complex songs they make during the mating season. Scientists are unsure why the males sing. Some believe it is a way of advertising themselves to females, while others hold that it allows migrating whales to stay in contact.

Each song lasts for 10 to 20 minutes and the males can sing continuously for 24 hours. At any period of time, all the males in a population sing the same song. A study, published in the journal Current Biology, shows that this song changes over time and spreads around the oceans. Dr. Ellen Garland, of Queensland University, said: "Our findings show cultural exchange on a vast scale. Songs move like cultural ripples from one population to another, causing all males to change their song to a new version."

Researchers recorded songs from six neighboring populations of whales in the Pacific over a decade. They found that new versions of the songs appear over time and always spread from west to east. It takes around two years for songs that appear in the waters off Australia to be heard in French Polynesia. Dr. Garland believes that a small number of whales may migrate to other populations carrying the new songs with them, or that they are heard by passing whales. Dr. Garland said, "We think this male search for song novelty is in the hope of being that little bit different and perhaps more attractive to the opposite sex."

Reading Exercises:

Check whether each statement is true (T) or false (F).

1. The author mentions Lady Gaga to prove the popularity of her hit singles.
2. The underlined word "release" in Paragraph 4 means " announce".
3. The discovery is very astonishing to experts, because it reveals the existence of cultural change.
4. Dr. Garland wants to tell us male whales adopt new songs to make themselves distinct.
5. It usually takes two years for songs that appear in the waters off Australia to be heard in French Polynesia.

New Words and Phrases

Text B:

humpback [ˈhʌmpbæk] *n.*A humpback or a humpback whale is a large whale with a curved back. 座头鲸

e.g. And this is the tail of the humpback whale.

隆背鲸鱼伸出了他的尾巴。

release [rɪˈliːs] *v.* to let sb./sth. come out of a place where they have been kept or trapped 释放

e.g. He was released from custody the next day.

第二天他从拘留所里放了出来。

四级真题中的使用：

1. The company just released an updated version last week, and it'll be utilized in over 50 undergraduate and graduate classrooms this coming school year.
2. In a press release describing the report, Mr. Annan stressed the need for the negotiations to focus on increasing the flow of money from rich to poor regions to help reduce their vulnerability to climate hazards while still curbing the emissions of the heat-trapping gases.

creature [ˈkriːtʃə(r)] *n.* any living thing that is not a plant,especially when it is of an unknown or unfamiliar kind 生物

The garden is surrounded by a hedge in which many small creatures can live.

花园四周是树篱，许多小动物可以在那里栖身。

mammal [ˈmæml] *n.* Any animal that gives birth to live babies, not eggs and feed its young on milk 哺乳动物

e.g. The function of a mammal's fur is to insulate the body.

哺乳动物皮毛的功能是使身体保温。

四级真题中的使用：

Human beings are a species of mammals.

astonish [əˈstɒnɪʃ] *v.*to surprise sb. very much 使吃惊

e.g. Her dedication constantly astonishes me.

她的奉献精神总是让我震惊。

四级真题中的使用：

1. That was partly due to his talents: showmanship, strategic vision, an astonishing attention to detail and a dictatorial management style which many bosses must have envied.
2. What was the most astonishing part of Mr. Jobs's success?

mating [ˈmeɪtɪŋ] *n.* sex between animals 交配

e.g. After mating the male wasps tunnel through the sides of their nursery.

交配之后，雄黄峰们就从蜂房的侧面钻出去了。

ripple [ˈrɪpl] *v.* to move or to make sth. move in very small waves 如波浪般起伏

e.g. It does not ripple like a brook in a garden.

它不像花园里的小溪那样潺潺汩汩。

be well-known for 因……闻名

e.g. While London could be known for its creative talent,what it still lacks is commercial clout.

虽然伦敦会因它的创造性的天赋而闻名，但它仍然缺少商业影响力。

on a vast scale 以一个巨大的规模

e.g. There will ultimately be six, and it will be like Homer's Epic, on a vast scale.

这里会有六部电影，这六部电影将会像一整部以更大规模展现的《荷马史诗》。

spread from 传播

e.g. The disease can spread from one mammalian species to another.

这种疾病能够在不同的哺乳类物种之间传播。

take around 带某人四处参观

e.g. During the morning your guide will take you around the city.

导游上午会带你们游览全城。

migrate to（尤指鱼、鸟）定期移栖到，洄游到，定期迁往

e.g. When did Asians begin to migrate to the United States?

亚洲人何时开始向美国移民的？

Writing

Part 1 命题分析

应用文 B

社会热点题材

1. 定义

社会热点题材指的是比较受广大群众关注的新闻和信息，或者指某个时期引人注目的社会现象及问题。与此题材相关的写作多以议论文为主，命题形式以文字提纲为主。

2. 写作步骤

基本结构：第一段提出社会问题或者描述社会现象。第二、三段为问题出现的原因或对自身生活和社会的影响，为文章的主体段落，要注意分层展开。

第一步：现象引申——提出观点。针对命题，概括性地提出所要论述的

社会问题和现象的主要特点。

第二步：找出、分析问题的原因或后果。说明问题产生的原因是什么，并且要分析说明原因造成的后果是什么。

第三步：提出建议或解决问题的方法，评论总结或对目前无法解决的问题提出展望。

3. 社会热点题材作文模板

社会热点题材模板按照开头、正文和结尾三个部分呈现，供同学们研究、模仿，以便快速提高此类作文的写作水平。

开头段：

（1）It has now drawn（increasing public / much nationwide）attention to the (issue / problem) of ________.

（2）Currently, ________ has been brought to such popular attention that ________.

（3）According to (a statistics / a survey / an investigation / a study / a poll), there is _________（提出问题）.

e.g. (Recently / Currently), the problem of global warming has been brought to such popular attention that governments at all levels place it on the top of the agenda.

According to the recent statistics, 80% teenagers are (addicted to / indulged in) playing online games.

正文段：

（1）（分析原因）The (phenomenon / problem / failure / change) (of / in) ________ is (partly / mainly / largely) (attributable to…/due to…/owing to…) ________. First of all, _________. Secondly, ________. Finally, ______.

（2）（分析原因）There are (several / many / a number of / a variety of) (causes / reasons / factors) could (account for / contribute to / lead to) (the dramatic growth / extraordinary development / inevitable change) in ________.

（3）（分析影响或结果）It is important for（people / teenagers）to realize that ________ will (produce / exert / have) a/an (remarkable / noticeable / striking / outstanding) (impact / influence / effect) on ________. In the first place, ________. In the second place, ________. Furthermore, __________.

结尾段：

（1）There is (no denying/little doubt) that (special / adequate / considerable / further) attention must be (paid / called / devoted) to the problem of _________. If we (ignore / are blind to) the problem, it is very likely that ________.

（2）It is high time that strict measures were taken to _______. (It is time that we laid considerable special emphasis on the growth _______.)

（3）It is (suggested / recommended / hoped) that (great / persistent / continuous) efforts should be made to reduce the risk of _______. Anyhow, (wider education / more publicity) should be given to the serious (consequences / effects) of ________.

（4）Accordingly, it is imperative for us to take drastic measures. To begin with, we should (appeal to the authorities to make strict laws to ______). In addition, we should (cultivate the awareness of people that _______ is essential to us). Only in this way can we (reverse the disturbing trend illustrated above).

Part 2 练习

Directions: *For this part, you are allowed 30 minutes to write a composition on the topic* ***Harmfulness of Fake Commodities****. You should write at least 120 words and you should base your composition on the outline (given in Chinese) below*:

（1）目前社会上有不少假冒伪劣商品（fake commodities）。为什么会有这种现象？

（2）举例说明假冒伪劣商品对消费者个人、社会等的危害。

【审题】本文属于提纲式文字命题。提纲第一点要求指出一种现象，并要求分析现象产生的原因；提纲第二点要求说明这种现象带来的影响，由此可判断本文应为现象解释类作文。

【中心思想】根据所给提纲，本文应包含以下内容：描述社会上存在很多假冒伪劣商品的现象，分析假冒伪劣商品泛滥的原因，说明假冒伪劣商品对消费者个人及社会等的危害。

【写作提纲】

Para. 1: The phenomenon of fake commodities

(1) Introduction to this phenomenon

(2) Reasons to the phenomenon of fake commodities

Para. 2: The negative effects of fake commodities

(1) The negative effects on individuals — illness

(2) The negative effects on society —unfair market, bad reputation

Para. 3: A conclusion

(1) cause — getting the same products with low price

(2) solution —eliminating fake commodities

【范文】

Harmfulness of Fake Commodities

Nowadays, there are many fake commodities in the marketplace, which range from daily commodities to expensive goods. Why are there so many fake ones? One reason is that people can make a bigger profit from selling fake commodities since their cost is lower than that of real ones. In addition, many consumers are willing to buy the cheaper products, which potentially stimulates the increase of fake commodities.

As everyone sees, fake commodities have brought negative effect on both the individual and the society. First of all, fake medicine and food threaten consumers' health seriously. For example, drinking fake alcohol may causes eye injuries. What's more, a large quantity of fake commodities in the marketplace causes unfair competition and puts the market economy in disorder. In addition, with so many Chinese fake commodities being exported overseas, the good reputation for goods made in China will be ruined.

No doubt, some fake commodities enable people to get the same products with low price. However, potential risks exist in these products. They destroy or harm what you already have, your health and even your life. All in all, we should make efforts to eliminate fake commodities in the market.

Vocabulary Exercises

A. *Fill in the blanks with the words in the box. Read the sentences carefully before making your choices. You may not use any of the words in the bank more than once. Change the form where necessary.*

dwarf ripple gravitational mammal astronomer release humpback creature astonish telescope mating spacecraft capture miscalculation

1. This interesting and charming____is unique to Borneo.
2. A____of laughter went through the audience.
3. He was____to see how his home town had changed in the past 10 years.
4. Like a____it has a curved mirror to collect the sunlight.
5. A neutron star has a____field strong enough to generate X-rays.
6. He had, from his second_____, a baby girl.
7. In children's stories, a______is an imaginary creature that is like a small man.
8. But I still haven't heard a good explanation for the___, so I ask Willetts to explain.
9. She had one eye and a_____.
10. A new star attracted the notice of the_____.
11. There is a close analogy between the gills of a fish and the lungs of a_____.
12. In thirty years from now the United States should have a manned_____on Mars.

B. *Fill in the blanks with the phrases in the box. Read the sentences carefully before making your choices. You may not use any of the phrases in the bank more than once. Change the form where necessary.*

be well-known for spread from take...around on the edge of shed light on turn into pick out turn out on a vast scale migrate to

1. I think I have got to stop or I might____a machine.
2. He____his political savvy and strong management skills.
3. Sometimes things don't_____the way we think they're going to.
4. The fire____the factory to the houses nearby.
5. Such missions could_____the origins of life in general.

6. I will___ three new plays particularly.

7. As parts of the world become uninhabitable, millions of people will try to______ more hospitable areas.

8. This movement has aroused the masses______.

9. A few snow-flakes were falling, and one, the largest of all, remained lying____a flower-pot.

10. Why don't you____him____and show him where everything is?

Extended Exercises

Cloze

There is a passage with 10 blanks. You are required to select one word for each blank from a list of choices in a word bank following the passage. Read the passage through carefully before making your choices. Each choice in the bank is identified by a letter.

A) absorb	B) combined	C) contribute	D) depth
E) emission	F) excursion	G) explore	H) floor
I) heights	J) indifferent	K) level	L) mixed
M) picture	N) unsure	O) voyage	

The ocean is heating up. That's the conclusion of a new study that finds that Earth's oceans now ___1___ heat at twice the rate they did 18 years ago. Around half of ocean heat intake since 1865 has taken place since 1997, researchers report online in Nature Climate Change.

Warming waters are known to ___2___ to coral bleaching（珊瑚白化）and they take up more space than cooler waters, raising sea ___3___. While the top of the ocean is studied, its depths are more difficult to ___4___. The researchers gathered 150 years of ocean temperature data in order to get better ___5___ of heat absorption from surface to seabed. They gathered together temperature readings collected by everything from a 19th century ___6___ of British naval ships to modern automated ocean probes. The extensive data sources, ___7___ with computer simulations（计算机模拟）, created a timeline of ocean temperature changes, including cooling from volcanic outbreaks and warming from fossil fuel __8__.

About 35 percent of the heat taken in by the oceans during the industrial era now resident at a __9__ of more than 700 meters, the researchers found. They say they're __10__ whether the deep-sea warming canceled out warming at the sea's surface.

Paragraph Matching

You are going to read a passage with ten statements attached to it. Each statement contains information given in one of the paragraphs. Identify the paragraph from which the information is derived. You may choose a paragraph more than once. Each paragraph is marked with a letter.

The Secret to Raising Smart Kids

[A] I first began to investigate the basis of human motivation - and how people persevere after setbacks-as a psychology graduate student at Yale University in the 1960s. Animal experiments by psychologists at the University of Pennsylvania had shown that after repeated failures, most animals conclude that a situation is hopeless and beyond their control. After such an experience an animal often remains passive even when it can effect change-a state they called learned helplessness.

[B] People can learn to be helpless, too. Why do some students give up when they encounter difficulty, whereas others who are no more skilled continue to strive and learn? One answer, I soon discovered, lay in people's beliefs about why they had failed.

[C] In particular, attributing poor performance to a lack of ability depresses motivation more than does the belief that lack of effort is to blame. When I told a group of school children who displayed helpless behavior that a lack of effort led to their mistakes in math, they learned to keep trying when the problems got tough. Another group of helpless children who were simply rewarded for their success on easier problems did not improve their ability to solve harm math problems. These experiments indicated that a focus on effort can help resolve helplessness and generate success.

[D] Later, I developed a broader theory of what separates the two general classes of learners-helpless versus mastery-oriented. I realized these different types of students not only explain their failures differently, but they also hold different "theories" of intelligence. The helpless ones believe intelligence is a fixed characteristic: you have only a certain amount, and that's that. I call this a "fixed mind-set（思维模式）". Mistakes crack their self-confidence because they attribute errors to a lack of ability, which they feel powerless to change. They avoid challenges because challenges make mistakes more likely. The mastery-orient children, on the other hand, think intelligence is not fixed and can be developed through education and hard work. Such children believe challenges are energizing rather than intimidating（令人生畏）；

[E] We validated these expectations in a study in which two other psychologists and I monitored 373 students for two years during the transition to junior high school, when the work gets more difficult and the grading more strict, to determine how their mind-sets might affect their math grades. At the beginning of seventh grade, we assessed the students' mind-sets by asking them to agree or disagree with statements such as "your intelligence is something very basic about you that you can't really change". We then assessed their beliefs about other aspects of learning and looked to see what happened to their grades.

[F] As predicted, the students with a growth mind-set felt that learning was a more important goal than getting good grades. In addition, they held hard work in high regard, they understood that even geniuses have to work hard. Confronted by a setback such as a disappointing test grade, students with a growth mind-set said they would study harder or try a different strategy. The students who held a fixed mind-set, however, were concerned about looking smart with less regard for learning. They had negative views of effort, believing that having to work hard was a sign of low ability. They thought that a person with talent or intelligence did not need to work hard to do well. Attributing a bad grade to their own lack of ability, those with a fixed mind-set said that they would study less in the future, try never to take that subject again and consider cheating on future tests.

[G] Such different outlook had a dramatic impact on performance. At the start of junior high, the math achievement test scores of the students with a growth mind-set were comparable to those of students who displayed a fixed mind-set. But as the work became more difficult, the students with a growth mind-set showed greater persistence. As a result, their math grades overtook those of the other students by the end of the first semester-and the gap between the two groups continued to widen during the two years we followed them.

[H] A fixed mind-set can also hinder communication and progress in the workplace and discourage or ignore constructive criticism and advice. Research shows that managers who have a fixed mind-set are less likely to seek or welcome feedback from their employees than are managers with a growth mind-set.

[I] How do we transmit a growth mind-set to our children? One way is by telling stories about achievements that result from hard work. For instance, talking about mathematical geniuses who were more or less born that way puts students in a fixed mind-set, but mathematicians who fell in love with math and developed amazing skills produce a growth mind-set.

[J] In addition, parents and teachers can help children by providing explicit instruction regarding the mind as a learning machine, I designed an eight-session workshop for 91 students whose math grades were declining in their first year of junior high. Forty-eight of the students received instruction in study skills only, whereas the others attended a combination of study skills sessions and classes in which they learned about the growth mind-set and how to apply it to schoolwork. In the growth mind-set classes, students read and discussed an article entitled "You Can Grow Your Brain." They were taught that the brain is like a muscle that gets stronger with use and that learning prompts the brain to grow new connections. From such instruction, many students began to see themselves as agents of their own brain development. Despite being unaware that there were two types of instruction, teachers reported significant motivational changes in 27% of the children in the growth mind-set workshop as compared with only 9% of students in the control group.

[K] Research is converging（汇聚）on the conclusion that great accomplishment and even genius is typically the result of years of passion and delication and not something that flows naturally from a gift.

1. The author's experiment shows that students with a fixed mind-set believe having to work hard is an indication of low ability.
2. Focusing on effort is effective in helping children overcome frustration and achieve success.
3. We can cultivate a growth mind-set in children by telling success stories that emphasize hard and work love of learning.
4. Students' belief about the cause of their failure explains their attitude toward setbacks.
5. In the author's experiment, students with a growth mind-set showed greater perseverance in solving difficult math problems.
6. The author conducted an experiment to find out about the influence of students' mind-sets on math learning.
7. After failing again and again, most animals give up hope.
8. Informing students about the brain as a learning machine is a good strategy to enhance their motivation for learning.
9. People with a fixed mind-set believe that one's intelligence is unchangeable.
10. In the workplace, feedback may not be so welcome to managers with a fixed mind-set.

Cultural Translation

Direction: *For this part, you are allowed 30 minutes to translate a passage from Chinese into English.*

随着中国的改革开放，如今很多年轻人都喜欢举行西式婚礼。新娘在婚礼上穿着白色婚纱，因为白色被认为是纯洁的象征。然而，在中国传统文化中，白色经常是葬礼上使用的颜色。因此务必记住，白花一定不要用作祝人康复的礼物，尤其不要送给老年人或危重病人。同样，礼金也不能装在白色信封里，而要装在红色信封里。

练习答案

Reading Exercises

Text A: 1 ～ 5 DCBBD

Text B: 1 ～ 5 FTTFT

Vocabulary Exercises

A:

1. creature
2. ripple
3. astonished
4. telescope
5. gravitational
6. mating
7. dwarf
8. miscalculation
9. humpback
10. astronomer
11. mammal
12. spacecraft

B:

1. turn into
2. is well-known for
3. turn out
4. spread from
5. shed light on
6. pick out
7. migrate to
8. on a vast scale
9. on the edge of

10. take...around

Extended Exercises

Cloze:

1 ~ 10: ACKGM OBEDN

Paragraph Matching:

1 ~ 10: FCIFG EAJDH

Cultural Translation:

With China's reform and opening up, many young people tend to hold Western-style weddings these days. The bride wears a white wedding dress at the wedding, because white is considered as a symbol of purity. However, in traditional Chinese culture, white is often used in funerals, so be sure to remember that white flowers must not be used as a gift to the patient, especially not to the seniors or patients in critical conditions. Similarly, the cash gift cannot be packed in a white envelope, but in a red envelope.

Unit 5 People Who Changed the Shape of Our World

Learning Objectives

After completing this unit, you will be able to do the following:

◇ Practice for the skill: How to identify key points;

◇ Grasp the main idea and the structure of the texts;

◇ Master the key languagc points and grammatical structure in the text;

◇ Conduct a series of reading, speaking and writing activities related to the theme in the unit.

Learning Difficult Points

In this unit, you will learn some difficult points listed below.

◇ Listening: How to identify key points.

◇ Writing: Applied Writing

Outline

The Following are the main sections in this Unit.

1. Listening
2. Speaking
3. Reading: Text A & Text B
4. Writing
5. Extended Exercises

Vocabulary

Listed below are some words appearing in this unit that you should make part of your vocabulary.

specify
adopt
stroke
permanent
characterize
remarkable
take in
stretch out
crowd into

Looking Ahead

People Who Changed the Shape of Our World

The world is a dangerous place to live, not because of the people who are evil, but because of the people who don't do anything about it.

— Albert Einstein

Introduction

Theodore Roosevelt served as the President of the United States from 1901 to 1909. He is famous for his domestic program Square Deal.

Japanese War was fought between the Russian Empire and the Empire of Japan over rival imperial ambitions. In 1905, Roosevelt persuaded the parties involved to meet in a peace conference in Portsmouth. His persistent and effective mediation led to the signing of the Treaty of Portsmouth, ending the war. The 1906 Nobel Peace Prize was awarded to Theodore Roosevelt for his efforts .

Roosevelt felt that a canal across the Isthmus of Panama would be beneficial for American military and commercial interests. After Colombia refused America's terms of building the canal, he supported the local political class in Panama in their quest to form an independent nation. He sent US warships to block sea lanes to thwart Colombia to suppress the rebellion. The new nation of Panama sold a canal zone to the US for $10 million and a steadily increasing yearly sum. Panama Canal was completed in 1914.

Speaking

Consider the following questions before reading:

1. Is there anyone that inspires you to face challenges?
2. Talk about a celebrity who you think highly of and his or her great contributions to the world.

Conversation

A: Do you know Shirley Temple?

B: Sure, she's a famous film star, especially when she is very young, before her 15.

A: Yes, her lovely appearance and performance impressed everyone. And at that time, the US was enduring a very severely economical crisis. Her film brought people hope and warmth, and encouraged millions of people who were in desperation.

B: She's so versatile that everybody loves her. She is a brilliant mimic.

A: Yes, but unfortunately, these children film stars always disappear when they grew up, when the applause dies.

B: Shirley Temple is an exception. She becomes an ambassador and keeps working for world peace, Poverty problems and diseases in developing countries. And as I know, her work is authorized by the United Union.

A: She is amazing!

UNIT 5 People Who Changed the Shape of Our World

Listening

Listening skills are fundamental to success in ENGLISH Listening. Through this part, we will have a detailed introduction to promote listening efficiency we could enhance by analyzing the three parts—News, Long conversation and Passage.

Listening Skills for Passage (1)

Keys to identify key points

Before listening, to obtain more information from the four options of a question, is essential in listening comprehension. Students can underline the special terms in the four choices, which help to know the figure, exact times, particular nouns, places and negative or positive meaning. For example, words with prefixes and suffixes always deserve attention. Students can underline prefixes such as dis-, in-, im-, il-, ir-, mis-, anti, un-; suffixes -less, -free, etc to predict the correct meaning. It is significant to mark the particular parts in the four options, for they will offer some implication for listening.

Example

Dogs, man's best friends, have a clear strategy for dealing with angry owners—they look away.

狗是人类最好的朋友，当主人愤怒时，它们有一个明确的战略来应对，那就是转移目光。

New research shows that dogs limit their eye contact with angry humans.

新的研究表明，狗限制自己与愤怒的人们有眼神接触。

The scientists suggest this may be an attempt to calm humans down.

科学家们认为这可能是为了让人类冷静下来。

This behavior may have evolved as dogs gradually learned they could benefit from avoiding conflicts with humans.

这种行为的发展可能是随着狗逐渐了解到它们可以从避免与人类的冲突中获益。

To conduct the tests, the University of Helsinki researchers trained 31 dogs to rest in front of a video screen.

为了进行这些测试，赫尔辛基大学的研究人员训练了31只狗在视频屏幕前休息。

Facial photos of dogs and humans were displayed on the screen for 1. 5 seconds.

狗和人的面部照片在屏幕上显示1. 5秒。

They showed threatening, pleasant and neutral expressions.

它们表现出威胁、愉快和中立的表情。

Nearby cameras tracked the dogs' eye movements.

附近的摄像机追踪记录了狗的眼球运动。

Dogs in the study looked most at the eyes of

Question 19.

A) They avoid looking at them.（avoid是对原文limit的同义替换。）

B) They run away immediately.

C) They show anger on their faces.

D) They make threatening sounds.

Question 20.

A) It turns to its owner for help.

B) It turns away to avoid conflict.

C) It looks away and gets angry, too.（focus是对原文中rest的同义替换。）

D) It focuses its eyes on their mouths.

humans and other dogs to sense their emotions.

研究中的狗几乎完全是通过看人类和其他狗的眼睛来感觉自己的情绪。

When dogs looked at expressions of angry dogs, their eyes rested more on the mouth, perhaps to interpret the threatening expressions.

当狗看着愤怒的狗时，它们的眼神更多地停留在嘴巴上，也许是为了中断那些带有威胁性的表情。

And when looking at angry humans, they tended to turn away their gaze.

当看着愤怒的人类时，它们倾向于转移目光。

Dogs may have learned to detect threat signs from humans and respond by trying to make peace, according to researcher Sanni Somppi.

根据研究人员 Sanni Somppi 的说法，狗可能已经学会检测来自人类的威胁信号，并通过试图达到和平来作出回应。

Avoiding conflicts may have helped dogs develop better bonds with humans.

避免冲突可能有助于狗与人类发展更好的联系。

The researchers also note that dogs scan faces as a whole to sense how people are feeling, instead of focusing on a given feature.

研究人员还指出，狗通过细看整个脸部以感知人们的感受，而不是专注于某个特征。

They suggest this indicates that dogs aren't sensing emotions from a single feature, but piecing together information from all facial features just as

Question 21.

A) By observing their facial features carefully.

B) By focusing on a particular body movement.

C) By taking in their facial expressions as a whole.（注意形容词 particular 和短语 as a whole。）

D) By interpreting different emotions in different ways.

humans do.

他们认为这表明狗不会从一个特征感知情绪，而是像人一样将所有面部特征的信息拼凑在一起。

Q19. What do dogs do when they are faced with angry humans?

Q20. What does a dog do when it sees the expressions of angry dogs?

Q21. How does a dog sense people's feelings?

Reading

Text A

Warming-up Activity:

Helen Keller

June 27 1880

An American author, political activist, and lecturer.

She was the first deafblind person to earn a Bachelor of Arts degree.

Helen Keller was a very intelligent woman who was afflicted at an early age in life. Her disabilities set in on her at eighteen months. As she grew older she didn't let her incapacity defeat her.

In 1933, Keller wrote an essay entitled, "Three Days To See". In this article

Keller gives a response about what she would like to see if she were given her sight back for three days. She also speaks about what it would be like if others were to lose their sight for three days as well.

Three Days to See

Helen Keller

All of us have read thrilling stories in which the hero had only a limited and specified time to live. Sometimes it was as long as a year; sometimes as short as twenty-four hours. But always we were interested in discovering just how the doomed man chose to spend his last days or his last hours. I speak, of course, of free men who have a choice, not condemned criminals whose sphere of activities is strictly delimited.

Such stories set us thinking, wondering what we should do under similar circumstances. What events, what experiences, what associations, should we crowd into those last hours as mortal beings? What happiness should we find in reviewing the past, what regrets?

Sometimes I have thought it would be an excellent rule to live each day as if we should die tomorrow. Such an attitude would emphasize sharply the values of life. We should live each day with a gentleness, a vigor, and a keenness of appreciation which are often lost when time stretches before us in the constant panorama of more days and months and years to come. There are those, of course, who would adopt the epicurean motto of “Eat, drink, and be merry”, but most people would be chastened by the certainty of impending death.

In stories, the doomed hero is usually saved at the last minute by some stroke of fortune, but almost always his sense of values is changed. He becomes more appreciative of the meaning of life and its permanent spiritual values. It has often been noted that those who live, or have lived, in the shadow of death bring a mellow sweetness to everything they do.

Most of us, however, take life for granted. We know that one day we must die, but usually we picture that day as far in the futurc. When we are in buoyant health, death is all but unimaginable. We seldom think of it. The days stretch out in an endless vista. So we go about our petty tasks, hardly aware of our listless attitude toward life.

The same lethargy, I am afraid, characterizes the use of all our facilities and senses. Only the deaf appreciate hearing, only the blind realize the manifold blessings that lie in sight. Particularly does this observation apply to those who have lost sight and hearing in adult life. But those who have never suffered impairment of sight or hearing seldom make the fullest use of these blessed faculties. Their eyes and ears take in all sights and sounds hazily.

Without concentration and with little appreciation, it is the same old story of not being grateful for what we have until we lose it, of not being conscious of health until we are ill.

I have often thought it would be a blessing if each human being were stricken blind and deaf for a few days at some time during his early adult life. Darkness would make him more appreciative of sight; silence would teach him the joys of sound.

Now and then I have tested my seeing friends to discover what they see. Recently I was visited by a very good friend who had just returned from a long walk in the woods, and I asked her what she had observed. "Nothing in particular." she replied. I might have been incredulous had I not been accustomed to such responses, for long ago I became convinced that the seeing see little.

How was it possible, I asked myself, to walk for an hour through the woods and see nothing worthy of note? I who cannot see find hundreds of things to interest me through mere touch. I feel the delicate symmetry of a leaf. I pass my hands lovingly about the smooth skin of a silver birch, or the rough, shaggy bark of a pine. In spring I touch the branches of trees hopefully in search of a bud, the first sign of awakening Nature after her winter's sleep. I feel the delightful, velvety texture of a flower, and discover its remarkable convolutions; and something of the miracle of Nature is revealed to me. Occasionally, if I am very fortunate, I place my hand gently on a small tree and feel the happy quiver of a bird in full song. I am delighted to have the cool waters of a brook rush through my open fingers. To me a lush carpet of pine needles or spongy grass is more welcome than the most luxurious

Persian rug. To me the pageant of seasons is a thrilling and unending drama, the action of which streams through my finger tips.

At times my heart cries out with longing to see all these things. If I can get so much pleasure from mere touch, how much more beauty must be revealed by sight. Yet, those who have eyes apparently see little. The panorama of color and action which fills the world is taken for granted. It is human, perhaps, to appreciate little that which we have and to long for that which we have not, but it is a great pity that in the world of light the gift of sight is used only as a mere convenience rather than as a means of adding fullness to life.

If I were the president of a university I should establish a compulsory course in "How to Use Your Eyes". The professor would try to show his pupils how they could add joy to their lives by really seeing what passes unnoticed before them. He would try to awake their dormant and sluggish faculties.

Reading Exercises:

1. The author talks about the dying heroes in thrilling stories to______.

A. show that a hero's life could either be short or long.

B. reveal that all of us are doomed to die.

C. make the values of life clear in a different way.

D. emphasize the importance of being a free man.

2. What can we infer from her friend's one-hour walk through the woods?

A.Her friend had observed nothing in particular.

B. Her friend didn't make the fullest use of her blessed eyes.

C. It's apparent that those who have eyes see little.

D.Her friend who takes the gift of sight for granted are expected to be more appreciative.

3. There are hundreds of things to interest Keller through mere touch in this passage except_____.

A. the delicate symmetry of a leaf

B. the most luxurious Persian rug

C. the smooth skin of a silver birch

D. the cool waters of a brook

4. The word — "incredulous" (line 3, paragraph 9) could be best replaced by______.

A. ashamed

B. suspicious

C. furious

D. rebellious

5. Why would Keller dream of establishing a course named "How to Use Your Eyes" in universities?

A. Because students are supposed to keep their eyes healthy.

B. Because professors try to add joy to their lives by adding a new course.

C. Because pupils long to acquire the knowledge about how to use eyes.

D. Because the varied blessings that lie in sight are worth noticing.

New Words and Phrases

Text A:

specify [ˈspesɪfaɪ] *v.* to state sth., especially by giving an exact measurement, time, exact instructions, etc. 具体说明；明确规定；详述；详列

e.g. Distance alone is insufficient to specify all properties at space.

单靠距离还不足以把空间的所有性质说清楚。

四级真题中的使用：

"We're asking the customers to specify what they want." said Craig Prusher, the chain's vice president of government relations.

adopt [əˈdɒpt] *v.* ① to take sb. else's child into your family and become its legal parent(s) 收养；领养 ② to start to use a particular method or to show a particular attitude towards sb./sth. 采用（某方法）；采取（某态度）③ to formally accept a suggestion or policy by voting 正式通过，表决采纳（建议、政策等）

e.g. Industry must adopt a much more proactive approach to formulating environmental policy.

企业必须更积极主动地制定环境政策。

四级真题中的使用：

1. Adopt a flexible approach to solving problems.
2. Familiar consumer products are being adopted by businesses, government and the armed forces.

stroke [strəʊk] *n*. ① an act of hitting a ball or a single movement of the arm when hitting sb./sth. 击球（动作）或（打、击等的）一下，一击 ② any of a series of repeated movements in swimming or rowing 划水动作；划桨动作 ③ a mark made by moving a pen, brush, etc. 笔画

e.g. Fill in gaps by using short, upward strokes of the pencil.

用铅笔向上短短地勾画几道来填充空白。

四级真题中的使用：

1. The authors documented an annual drop of as many as 120000 cases of heart disease, 66000 instances of stroke and 99000 heart attacks caused by high blood pressure after a 3-g-per-day reduction in salt.
2. You would not be surprised if a stranger tried to shake hands when you were introduced, but you might be a little startled if they bowed, started to stroke you or kissed you on both cheeks.
3. Anyone who has patted a dog, stroked a cat, sat under a tree with a pint of beer, given or received a bunch of flowers or chosen to walk through the park on a nice day, understands that.

permanent [ˈpɜːmənənt] *adj*. lasting for a long time or all time in the future; existing all the time 永久的；永恒的；

e.g. Heavy drinking can cause permanent damage to the brain.

酗酒能造成永久性大脑损伤。

四级真题中的使用：

1. Such books, which only rarely end up in permanent collections, either private or public, will probably only be available as e-books within a few years.
2. His doctors were puzzled by the strange case of permanent sleeplessness.
3. The bid went instead to Fuji, which exploited its sponsorship to win a permanent foothold in the marketplace.

characterize [ˈkærəktəraɪz] *v*. ① to be typical of a person, place or thing 是……的

特征；以……为典型② to give sth. its typical or most noticeable qualities or features 使……具有特点③ to describe or show the qualities of sb./sth. in a particular way 描述，刻画……的特征

e.g. A bold use of color characterizes the bedroom.

这间卧室的特点是用色大胆。

四级真题中的使用：

1. Under these circumstances, it's natural to look for what may appear to be the most "practical" way out of the problem "Major in a subject designed to get you a job" seems the obvious answer to some, though this ignores the fact that many disciplines in the humanities characterized as "soft" often, in fact, lead to employment and success in the long run.
2. What characterizes a knowledge economy according to the passage?
3. Disputes were characterized by intense verbal（言语上的）aggression, tended to be repeated and not resolved and made men, more than women, extremely angry.

remarkable [rɪˈmɑ:kəbl] *adj*. unusual or surprising in a way that causes people to take notice

e.g. Western businessmen are showing remarkable prudence in investing in the region.

西方商人在向该地区投资时表现出非同一般的深谋远虑。

四级真题中的使用：

1. Remarkable changes have taken place in the book business.
2. But the remarkable thing is how well the system usually works.

reveal [rɪˈvi:l] *v*. ① to make sth. known to sb. 揭示；显示；透露② to show sth. that previously could not be seen 显出；展示

e.g.The statistics don't reveal of course unrecorded crime.

这项统计数据显然没有披露未登记的罪案。

四级真题中的使用：

A recent survey by a credit bureau revealed that the number of alarmed citizens had shot up to 76 percent.

speak of 谈到，讲到；显示出……

e.g. When we speak of unity, we do not mean unprincipled peace.

所谓和平，并非无原则的和气。

take in 吸收；领会；欺骗；接待

e.g. I know I was a naive fool to trust him but he is a real charmer who totally took me in.

我知道我当初幼稚无知，竟然信任他，可是他真是迷人，把我完全给骗了。

crowd into（使）充满某空间；涌现于（某人）的脑海

e.g. He managed to crowd into the train.

他总算挤上了火车。

stretch out 延伸；满足需要

e.g. She would be able to stretch out her cramped limbs and rest for a few hours.

她将能伸展一下蜷缩的四肢，休息几个小时。

be conscious of 知道；意识；察觉；

e.g. Make time for exercise and be conscious of your diet.

腾出时间锻炼身体并注意你的饮食。

Text B

Warming-up Activity:

The Walt Disney Company is one of the largest media and entertainment corporations in the world. Founded on October 16,1923, by brothers Walt and Roy Disney as a small animation studio, it became one of the biggest Hollywood studios and owns several television networks, including the American Broadcasting Company (ABC).

At this time, Disney have produced over 100 films through their studios and also under the label of other studios such as Touchstone Pictures and Hollywood Pictures. Many of these are critically acclaimed and very popular, including classic

animated movies such as *Beauty and the Beast*. More recently they have founded websites such as Go.com. and also television channels such as the Disney Channel.

Walt: The Man behind the Myth

Shortly after, Walt got a job at Piesman Reubin art studio.While at Piesman Reubin, he met a quiet but highly talented young man named Abe Iwerks. The two young men started a little company of their own.

"They weren't able to, to make much of a living with their reels and sometimes rarely making enough to get by, and, then, they saw an ad in the paper for the Kansas City Slide Company. And so Walt left Abe to run the partnership, and he was hired. And, eventually, Abe joined him there ."

It was a Kansas city film maker that Walt was first introduced to animated films — cartoons.

Walt Disney (CBC Interview, 1963)

"Of course they were very crude things then and, also a little puppet things. We didn't draw them like we do today. I used it to make a little cut— out things, and joint through pin and we put them to the camera, and move and maneuver, make them do things."

Walt spent hours at the Kansas City Library, learning about animation. It was here that he came across a nineteen-century book by a British artist named Edward Moboridge on animal and human local motion.

Chuck Jones (Animation Producer)

"People don't notice that the term 'animation' was first noticed by a man named Noah Webster, (and he) was writing a dictionary in 1837. And he ran across this word 'animation' , and he wrote under it : 'to evoke life'."

Charles Solomon (Author and Historian)

"Well, in the America, during the 20s, the animation industry was really centered on New York city. That's where the first studios have been established and that's where the great majority of them still were. At that time, there were an enormous amount of silent, one-reel comedies being put on, to show in the movie theaters."

Walt took a borrowed camera to the shed behind his house and began making cartoons of his own. He called them 'Laugh-O-Grams', and sold the first one to the Newman Theater in Kansas City.

J. B. Kaufman (Author and Historian)

"And one of the great things about that, I think, is that it opens with a wonderful shot of Walt Disney sitting at his drawing board. This is Walt Disney at the beginning of his journey, and we have a privilege to glance over it. It wasn't long before he moved out of animation and have other people working with him in the actual drawing pictures, but this is one segment that we can say is fully animated by Walt Disney himself."

"I think he really wants to get into full animation and he realized just from the laborious nature of little short scenes like the police station scene, and that, this was not something that one person wanted to do, alone. So that's why he went to recruit people to start the 'Laugh-O-Grams' company, and they made films which are referred to as today's modernized fairy tales. Basically what they did was to take a fairy tale but then do a contemporary spin on it. So when he does his version of 'Puss in Boots' for example, this is the cat with his master going to the movies and then seeing a parody of the latest Rudolf Valentino picture."

These were just a bunch of kids, they don't have a worldwide organization behind them; these were a bunch of boyhood friends who have developed a common interest in animated cartoons and want to give it a whirl. So they are doing things by trial and error, they are learning techniques as they go along. And you get to see them doing that as you watch the films. It's very promptive and it's, it's, um, just a lot of fun.

Dorothy Puder (Niece)

"I was carrying a full milk bottle, and then he reversed the film, so that I backed up, the milk all came up into the bottle, that was one little film that we did."

Roy developed tuberculosis, and was sent to a sanatorium; Herbert and his family were transferred by the postal service to a new job in Portland Oregon; Elias and Flora decided to pin them for a lender as well. The crowded house on Belfountain, fell empty. One morning, Walt accompanied his parents and his sister Ruth to the Kansas city Union Station for a tearful farewell.

The Letter from Walt's Sister Ruth

"When Walt took us to the train, I never knew Walt's emotions much, but he couldn't keep his face straight, he sadly turned and left. He was upset, very upset. He realized that he was going to be alone then."

On May 23rd, 1922, Walt officially incorporated the "Laugh-O-Grams" films in a two-room suit in McConaughey building. He was twenty years old.

J. B. Kaufman(Author and Historian)

When Victorial clubs signed the contract for the "Laugh-O-Grams", the contract specified that Disney and his co-workers will get 11100 dollars, but what they got is 100 dollars. That was it. The contract was set up to say, they were supposed to get the rest of the money a long way down the road, but conveniently enough, Victorial clubs went out of business before that. I think a lot of people would be tempted to become very conservative and do something easy and safe, What Disney does is to go out and blow out on the most lavish film you can possibly make. And it was called *Alice in Wonderland*.

Charles Solomon (Author and Historian)

"Well, A number of people have been experimenting during the 20s with live action and animation combinations, but the standard way of doing that which Flychise has pioneered was to put an animated character into a live action world. Walt reversed it to create something new, something different, very typically, and put the live action character into the animated world, which rarely have been done before or done very little. In the first part of the film, she goes into the cartoon studio, so you get this kind of wonderful, quizzical look at a cartoon studio through a child's eyes."

Virginia Davis (Actress)

"The name of the first film which was a test film that he used was called *Alice in Wonderland*, and it was shot in my mother's house, at least the live action part of it. And that is where he introduced the idea of 'cartoons'. And when I came home, I was to be put to bed, and then I dreamed the whole sequence of the Alice' s cartoons, and he said, you know, "Run, move you arms, move you arms, like you're running..."

Half way into the production, Walt was broke, "Laugh-O-Grams" went out of business. In July, 1923, Walt sold his movie camera. He would go where all the makers go. He would head for Hollywood.

Reading Exercises:

Check whether each statement is true (T) or false (F).

1. Walt and Abe Iwerks are both fired by the Kansas City Slide Company.
2. "Animation" was first noticed by a British artist on animal and human local motion.
3. Disney and his co-workers got 11100 dollars based on the contract that Victorial clubs signed for the "Laugh-O-Grams".
4. It was Flychise who has pioneered to animated character into a live action world.
5. Walt introduced the idea of 'cartoons' when a test film called *Alice in Wonderland* was shot in the house of Virginia's mother.

New Words and Phrases

Text B:

crude[kru:d] *adj*. ① simple and not very accurate but giving a general idea of sth. 粗略的；大概的② simply made, not showing much skill or attention to detail 粗糙的；粗制的③ offensive or rude, especially about sex 冒犯的；粗俗的（尤其有关性的）④ (of oil and other natural substances) in its natural state, before it has been treated with chemicals 天然的；自然的

e.g. He was critical of the people, disparaging of their crude manners.

他对那些人很有看法，看不起他们粗俗的举止。

四级真题中的使用：

It wants to expand its storage of crude oil.

motion [ˈməʊʃn] *n.* ① the act or process of moving or the way sth. moves 运动；移动 ② a formal proposal that is discussed and voted on at a meeting 动议；提议

e.g. Such a motion is considered a test of backbench opinion.

这样的动议被视为对后座议员立场的考验。

四级真题中的使用：

Although no form of matter yet discovered moves as fast as or faster than light, scientific experiments have already confirmed that accelerated motion causes a traveler's time to be stretched.

shed [ʃed] *n.* ① a small piece of building, usually built of wood or metal, used for keeping things in 简易房，棚（用于贮藏物品）② a large industrial building, used for working in or keeping equipment（工业上用于生产或存放设备的）厂房，工棚，库房 *v.* to get rid of sth. 去除；摆脱

e.g. He made his way along a well-trodden path towards the shed.

他顺着一条常有人走的小路走向小屋。

四级真题中的使用：

Since 2007 America has shed 5 million jobs.

spin [spɪn] *v.* ① to turn round and round quickly; to make sth. do this（使）快速旋转 ② to make thread from wool, cotton, silk, etc. by twisting it 纺（线）；纺（纱）*n.* a very fast turning movement 高速旋转

e.g. Set on a cool wash and finish with a short spin.

设定用凉水洗衣，最后短时脱水。

reverse [rɪˈvɜːs] *v.* to change sth. completely so that it is the opposite of what it was before 颠倒；使完全相反 *n.* the opposite of what has just been mentioned 相反的情况（或事物）*adj.* opposite to what had been mentioned 反面的

e.g. His answer was just the reverse of what I expected.

他的回答正好与我期望的相反。

pioneer[ˌpaɪəˈnɪə(r)] *v.* when sb. pioneers sth., they are one of the first people to do, discover or use sth. new 当开拓者；做先锋；倡导 *n.* a person who is the first to study and develop a particular area of knowledge, culture, etc. that other people then continue to develop 先驱；带头人

e.g. Li Dazhao was a pioneer of the Chinese revolution.

李大钊是中国革命的先驱。

get by 通过；设法；过得去；继续存在

e.g. No one is able to get by without oxygen.

没有氧气人不能维持生命。

come across 偶遇；偶然发现；使产生……印象

e.g. This is the worst place I've come across.

这是我去过的最差的地方。

put on 增加；穿上；上演；使运转

e.g. She was so ill that she was put on a respirator.

她病得很严重，戴上了人工呼吸器。

glance over 浏览；翻阅

e.g. She saw him glance over her slim and erect carriage.

她看到他快速地朝她苗条而挺拔的身姿瞥了一眼。

refer to 涉及；指的是；用于；参考

e.g.There's the original to refer to.

有原文可参照。

back up < 篮球 > 协防，补防；支持；堵塞；复制；往后退

e.g. Clogged pipes caused drain water to back up into the room.

水管堵塞，排出去的水倒灌入室。

blow out 吹熄；爆裂；吹出；停吹

e.g. Make a wish and blow out the candles on your cake.

许个愿吧，把蛋糕上的蜡烛都吹灭。

Writing

Part 1 命题分析

应用文 C

观点论证类

1. 定义

观点论证类作文要求考生针对题目所给论点，按照提纲要求，通过摆事实、讲道理的方式对论点进行论证。

2. 写作步骤

基本提纲结构：第一段通过现象、背景介绍引出话题（公众观点 + 大概理由）。第二段阐述关于话题的相关因素（影响、作用、好处、危害或原因等）。第三段陈述自己的观点或展望未来。

3. 观点论证型作文模板

观点论证型模板按照开头、正文和结尾三个部分呈现，供同学们研究、模仿，以便快速提高此类作文的写作水平。

提出观点段：

①论点背景。②“It is true that...”，提出论点。③“No one can deny that...”，正确地表现出。④“Therefore”，重申论点。

论证观点段：

⑤“Many remarkable reasons contribute to this argument.”⑥“First of all”，论据一。⑦“For example”，支持论据一的事例。⑧“Besides...”，论据二。⑨“In addition...”，论据三。

总结观点段：

⑩“All mentioned above tells us that”，重申观点。⑪“Therefore, there is no denying that...”，正确态度或做法。⑫“In a word”，观点总结。

Part 2 练习

Directions: *For this part, you are allowed 30 minutes to write a composition on the topic* **Practice Makes Perfect**. *You should write at least 120 words and you should base your composition on the outline (given in Chinese) below:*

（1）怎样理解“熟能生巧”

（2）例如：在英语学习中……

（3）又如……

【审题】本题属于提纲式文字命题。提纲第一点要求解释一个成语，提纲第二点和第三点要求举例论证该成语的正确性，由此可判断本文应为观点论证类作文。

【中心思想】根据所给提纲，本文应包含以下内容：阐释“熟能生巧”的含义和道理；举例说明该成语在英语学习中以及其他方面的应用；重申“熟能生巧”的意义，总结全文。

【写作提纲】

Para. 1: Introduction

(1) the proverb — “Practice makes perfect”

(2) The deep and profound significance of the saying

Para. 2: Examples contributing to this proverb

(1) Extra practice to learn English well

a. Reading English books

b. Listening to English broadcast

c. Communicating with foreigners

(2) Being skilled at computer operation

Para. 3: Suggestions: Two vital factors to achieve success

a. Continuous practice and efforts

b. A right theoretical direction

【范文】

Practice Makes Perfect

“Practice makes perfect”, is a proverb full of logic, which has been generally accepted. It tells us that skill comes by exercise and proficiency comes from familiarity.

Many remarkable examples contribute to this argument. For one example, in order to learn English well, we should practice as much as possible. We need read English books, listen to English broadcast, communicate with foreign friends so as to pass CET4 and CET6 in college. For another example, if we want to be skilled at using computers, we need keep practicing and make computers run efficiently. Moreover, in other fields, practice is also necessary and we can hardly do things well without practice and preparation in advance.

From what mentioned above, we might draw the conclusion that continuous practice leads to proficiency. But what is worth noting is that if there is no right theoretical direction, we might go in the wrong direction. Therefore,using practice and theory to develop skill would be much better.

Vocabulary Exercises

A. *Fill in the blanks with the words in the box. Read the sentences carefully before making your choices. You may not use any of the words in the bank more than once. Change the form where necessary.*

crude stroke characterize reveal shed spin motion specify pioneer permanent adopt reverse remarkable

1. It didn't rain, which turned out to be a_____of luck.
2. Please read the names on this list in_____order.
3. Strange shadows moved silently in the almost____darkness.
4. This is the virus in very____simple diagrammatic form.
5. In no way am I going to______any of his methods.
6. There was a_____resemblance between him and Pete.
7. Several different names have emerged to____different parts of the spectrum.
8. Companies should be made to___more about their financial position.
9. The regulations____that you may use a dictionary in the examination.
10. I have set the wheels in_____to sell Endsleigh Court.
11. A lorry piled with scrap metal had_____its load.
12. The boat started to____around in the water.
13. He acted as_____in proposing the method.

B. *Fill in the blanks with the phrases in the box. Read the sentences carefully before making your choices. You may not use any of the phrases in the bank more than* *once. Change the form where necessary.*

be conscious of	speak of	come across	back up	refer to	take in	stretch out
put on	blow out	glance over	get by	crowd into		

1. This is nothing to____.
2. He stopped to____the misty lake where water joined the sky.
3. Does your remark____all of us?
4. Fish____oxygen through their gills.
5. This reminds you to always____the actions you're taking.
6. ____the candles and make a wish.
7. You can enjoy the extraordinary sight unbroken cloud plains that____before you.
8. We must hang in whenever we____difficulties.
9. Thomas managed to____on a small amount of money.
10. The bus had to____and turn around.
11. They had managed to____train.
12. Even clever people are not terribly clever when____the spot.

Extended Exercises

Cloze

There is a passage with 10 blanks. You are required to select one word for each blank from a list of choices in a word bank following the passage. Read the passage through carefully before making your choices. Each choice in the bank is identified by a letter.

A) arrived	B) consuming	C) direct	D) exclusively
E) including	F) inform	G) raw	H) reached
I) relatively	J) remains	K) resources	L) staple
M) suggest	N) surprising	O) test	

The method for making beer has changed over time. Hops（啤酒花）, for example, which give many a modern beer its bitter flavor, are a ___1___ recent addition to the beverage. This was first mentioned in reference to brewing in the ninth century.

Now, researchers have found a ___2___ ingredient in residue（残留物）from 5000-year-old beer brewing equipment. While digging two pits at a site in the central plains of China, scientists discovered fragments from pots and vessels. The different shapes of the containers ___3___ they were used to brew, filter, and store beer. They may be ancient "beer-making tools", and the earliest ___4___ evidence of beer brewing in China, the researchers reported in the Proceedings of the National Academy of Sciences. To ___5___ that theory, the team examined the yellowish, dried ___6___ inside the vessels. The majority of the grains, about 80%, were from cereal crops like barley（大麦）, and about 10% were bits of roots, ___7___ lily, which would have made the beer sweeter, the scientists say. Barley was an unexpected find; the crop was domesticated in Western Eurasia and didn't become a ___8___ food in central China until about 2000 years ago, according to the researchers. Based on that timing, they indicate barley may have ___9___ in the region not as food, but as ___10___ material for beer brewing.

Paragraph Matching

You are going to read a passage with ten statements attached to it. Each statement contains information given in one of the paragraphs. Identify the paragraph from which the information is derived. You may choose a paragraph more than once. Each paragraph is marked with a letter.

The Blessing and Curse of the People Who Never Forget

A handful of people can recall almost every day of their lives in enormous detail and after years of research neuroscientists are finally beginning to understand how they do it.

[A] For most of us, memory is a mess of blurred and faded pictures of our lives. As much as we would like to cling on to our past, even the saddest moments can be washed away with time.

[B] Ask Nima Veiseh what he was doing for any day in the past 15 years, however, and he will give you the details of the weather, what he was wearing, or even what side of the train he was sitting on his journey to work. "My memory is like a library of video tapes, walk-throughs of every day of my life from waking to sleeping." he explains.

[C] Veiseh can even put a date on when those tapes started recording: 15 December 2000, when he met his first girlfriend at his best friend's 16th birthday party. He had always had a good memory, but the thrill of young love seems to have shifted a gear in his mind: from now on, he would start recording his whole life in detail. "I could tell you everything about every day after that. "

[D] Needless to say, people like Veiseh are of great interest to neuroscientists（神经科学专家）hoping to understand the way the brain records our lives. A couple of recent papers have finally opened a window on these people's extraordinary minds. And such research might even suggest ways for us all to relive our past with greater clarity.

[E] "Highly superior autobiographical memory" (or HSAM for short), first came to light in the early 2000s, with a young woman named Jill Price. Emailing the neuroscientist and memory researcher Jim McGaugh one day, she claimed that she could recall every day of her life since the age of 12. Could he help explain her experiences?

[F] McGaugh invited her to his lab, and began to test her: he would give her a date and ask her to tell him about the world events on that day. True to her word, she was correct almost every time.

[G] It didn't take long for magazines and documentary film-makers to come to understand her "total recall", and thanks to the subsequent media interest, a few dozen other subjects (including Veiseh) have since come forward and contacted the team at the University of California, Irvine.

[H] Interestingly, their memories are highly self-centred: although they can remember "autobiographical" life events in extraordinary detail, they seem to be no better than average at recalling impersonal information, such as random（任意选取的）lists of words. Nor are they necessarily better at remembering a round of drinks, say. And although their memories are vast, they are still likely to suffer from "false memories". Clearly, there is no such thing as a "perfect" memory—their extraordinary minds are still using the same flawed tools that the rest of us rely on. The question is, how?

[I] Lawrence Patihis at the University of Southern Mississippi recently studied around 20 people with HSAM and found that they scored particularly high on two measures: fantasy proneness（倾向）and absorption. Fantasy proneness could be considered a tendency to imagine and daydream, whereas absorption is the tendency to allow your mind to become fully absorbed in an activity—to pay complete attention to the sensations（感受）and the experiences. "I'm extremely sensitive to sounds, smells and visual detail." explains Nicole Donohue, who has taken part in many of these studies. "I definitely feel things more strongly than the average person. "

[J] The absorption helps them to establish strong foundations for recollection, says Patihis, and the fantasy proneness means that they revisit those memories again and again in the coming weeks and months. Each time this initial memory trace is "replayed", it becomes even stronger. In some ways, you probably go through that process after a big event like your wedding day—but the difference is that thanks to their other psychological tendencies, the HSAM subjects are doing it day in, day out, for the whole of their lives.

[K] Not everyone with a tendency to fantasise will develop HSAM, though, so Patihis suggests that something must have caused them to think so much about their past. "Maybe some experience in their childhood meant that they became obsessed（着迷）with calendars and what happened to them." says Patihis.

[L] The people with HSAM I've interviewed would certainly agree that it can be a mixed blessing. On the plus side, it allows you to relive the most transformative and enriching experiences. Veiseh, for instance, travelled a lot in his youth. In his spare time, he visited the local art galleries, and the paintings are now lodged deep in his autobiographical memories.

[M] "Imagine being able to remember every painting, on every wall, in every gallery space, between nearly 40 countries." he says. "That's a big education in art by itself." With this comprehensive knowledge of the history of art, he has since become a professional painter.

[N] Donohue, now a history teacher, agrees that it helped during certain parts of her education: “I can definitely remember what I learned on certain days at school. I could imagine what the teacher was saying or what it looked like in the book.”

[O] Not everyone with HSAM has experienced these benefits, however. Viewing the past in high definition can make it very difficult to get over pain and regret. “It can be very hard to forget embarrassing moments.” says Donohue. “You feel the same emotions—it is just as raw, just as fresh... You can’t turn off that stream of memories, no matter how hard you try. ” Veiseh agrees: “It is like having these open wounds—they are just a part of you.” he says.

[P] This means they often have to make a special effort to lay the past to rest. Bill, for instance, often gets painful “flashbacks”, in which unwanted memories intrude into his consciousness, but overall he has chosen to see it as the best way of avoiding repeating the same mistakes. “Some people are absorbed in the past but not open to new memories, but that’s not the case for me. I look forward to each day and experiencing something new.”

1. People with HSAM have the same memory as ordinary people when it comes to impersonal information.
2. Fantasy proneness will not necessarily cause people to develop HSAM.
3. Veiseh began to remember the details of his everyday experiences after he met his first young love.
4. Many more people with HSAM started to contact researchers due to the mass media.
5. People with HSAM often have to make efforts to avoid focusing on the past.
6. Most people do not have clear memories of past events.
7. HSAM can be both a curse and a blessing.
8. A young woman sought explanation from a brain scientist when she noticed her unusual memory.
9. Some people with HSAM find it very hard to get rid of unpleasant memories.
10. A recent study of people with HSAM reveals that they are liable to fantasy and full absorption in an activity.

Cultural Translation

Directions: *For this part, you are allowed 30 minutes to translate a passage from Chinese into English.*

黄河是亚洲第三、世界第六长的河流。“黄”这个字描述的是其河水浑浊的颜色。黄河发源于青海，流经 9 个省份，最后注入渤海。黄河是中国赖以生存的几条河流之一。黄河流域（river basin）是中国古代文明的诞生地，也是中国早期历史上最繁荣的地区。然而，由于极具破坏力的洪水频发，黄河曾造成多次灾害。在过去的几十年里，政府采取了各种措施防止灾害发生。

练习答案

Reading Exercises

Text A: 1 ～ 5 CDBBD

Text B: 1 ～ 5 TFFTT

Vocabulary Exercises

A:

1. stroke
2. reverse
3. permanent
4. crude
5. adopt
6. remarkable
7. characterize
8. reveal
9. specify
10. motion
11. shed
12. spin
13. pioneer

B:

1. speak of
2. glance over
3. refer to
4. take in
5. be conscious of
6. Blow out
7. stretch out
8. come across

9. get by
10. back up
11. crowd into
12. put on

Extended Exercises

Cloze:

1 ～ 10: INMCO JELAG

Paragraph Matching:

1 ～ 10: HKCGP ALEOI

Cultural Translation:

The Yellow River is the third longest in Asia and the sixth longest in the world. "Yellow" describes the color of the muddy river. The river originates in Qinghai, and runs through nine provinces before it empties into the Bohai Sea. The Yellow River is one of the several rivers that sustain life and livelihood in China. The Yellow River basin is the cradle of China's ancient civilization and was once the most prosperous region in early history of China. However, the Yellow River caused many disasters due to frequent catastrophic floods. Hence over the past several decades, the Chinese government has taken various measures to prevent such disasters.

Unit 6 Moral Values

Learning Objectives

After completing this unit, you will be able to do the following:

◇ Practice for the skill: How to identify synonyms;

◇ Grasp the main idea and the structure of the texts;

◇ Master the key language points and grammatical structure in the text;

◇ Conduct a series of reading, speaking and writing activities related to the theme in the unit.

Learning Difficult Points

In this unit, you will learn some difficult points listed below.

◇ Listening: How to identify synonyms.

◇ Writing: Applied Writing

Outline

The Following are the main sections in this Unit.

1. Listening
2. Speaking
3. Reading: Text A & Text B
4. Writing
5. Extended Exercises

Vocabulary

Listed below are some words appearing in this unit that you should make part of your vocabulary.

plead
clinch
inclination
trustworthy
fall apart
apt to
restrain from
silverware
envision

Looking Ahead

Moral Values

Morality is not the conscience of the despicable means, but the struggle and hardship, passion and pain.

—Thomas Man

Morality is not really the doctrine of how to make ourselves happy but of how we are to be worthy of happiness.

—Immanuel Kant

Introduction

Almost everything changes through time in the world. However, the moral value of humanity will never change.

Most people today will probably think that moral is valueless. If moral value is truly worthless, the world exists colorless full of discrimination and killing. Money isn't the root cause of these problems. The real reason is the lack of moral values.

Individuals tend to do what the majority are doing. They believe many people are making the same mistake, which can be forgivable. If you don't encourage or promote moral values in life, you will lose it in the end. You may not suffer now, but the next generation may suffer. When too many people think that morals are valueless, then those values will ultimately disappear.

Speaking

Consider the following questions before reading:

1. What is the difference between a true friend and fake friend?
2. What's your understanding of moral values?

Conversation

Study and practice the conversation below.

A: Do Americans have any morals?

B: That's a good question. Many people insist that ideas about right and wrong are merely personal opinions. Some voices, though, are calling Americans back to traditional moral values. Have you heard *The Book of Virtues* in 1993? The author, William J. Bennett, shows that many Americans still believe in moral values in the book.

A: But why are they like this now?

B: To begin with, moral values in America are like those in any culture. But different cultures influenced how people show these virtues.

A: So it is not illegal for Americans to authorize the NSA to monitor the international calls and e-Mails secretly and to be an integral part of the U.S. war on terror. Right?

B: The idea made by the government; it doesn't mean all U.S. citizens think so. Besides, should not each country fight the terrorist forces to safeguard its national security?

A: However, there are also representatives of various parties involved in the decision-making process. I support the fight against terrorist forces. And it is our responsibility, but I think it can be conducted in a legitimate way.

B: Maybe you are right. The U.S. government should fight against terrorism on a firm leagal footing.

UNIT 6 Moral Values

Listening

Listening skills are fundamental to success in English Listening. Through this part, we will have a detailed introduction to promote listening efficiency we could enhance by analyzing the three parts—News, Long conversation and Passage.

Listening Skills for Passage (2)

Keys to identify Synonyms:

In order to detect students' vocabulary, thc device of employing synonyms is frequently used in listening comprehension. Synonym refers to word or phrase with the same meaning as another in the same language, though perhaps with a different style, grammar or technical use.

When a word or phrase in the option is synonymous with one in passage, very often than not, this word or phrase could be the answer. Detecting and recognizing synonymous words and phrases is essential to help understand the passage and match the information.

Example（出自四级听力原文）

Catherine loved Facebook. With Facebook she could stay connected with her family no matter how faraway they were.

Catherine 很喜欢脸书。有了脸书，不管她和她的家人相距多远都可以随时保持联络。

She could see their photos and read their status updates.

她可以看到她家人的照片以及状态更新。

With Facebook she could keep her relatives up to date on what she was doing.

有了脸书，她可以让亲戚了解她在做什么。

Another thing Catherine loved about Facebook was that she didn't have to think about time zones when updating family.

Catherine 很爱脸书的另外一点就是，她看她家人发的状态时也不用考虑时差。

Whenever she called her parents or other relatives,she always had to think about the time difference so that she wouldn't wake someone up or call when she knew they were in church.

每当她给父母或其他亲戚打电话时，她总得考虑时差不同，以免吵醒了谁或打扰到正在做礼拜的人。

Facebook was so convenient.

脸书是如此方便。

When Catherine joined Facebook, some of her classmates at high school started to add her as a friend.

Catherine 刚用脸书的时候，她的一些高中同学也加她为好友了。

At first, this didn't bother her.

一开始这对她并没有什么影响。

She loved learning about the success of people she knew when she was just a teenager.

她乐于了解她在十几岁时就认识的同学现在的成功。

She loved finding out people were getting

The answer to Question 19 can be found here for the synonymous phrase: particular convenience that She could update her family any time she liked.

The answer to Question 20 can be found here for the synonymous sentence: She enjoyed reading her friends' status updates.

married, having babies and traveling.

她也喜欢了解谁结婚了，谁怀孕了，谁去旅行了。

Soon, however, Catherine found herself comparing herself with the people she was reading about on Facebook.

但是不久后，她发现自己在和她在脸书上了解的人作比较。

It began to make her feel bad that some people seemed to be doing so much better than she was.

当她看到脸书上的朋友过得比她好很多时，她觉得不开心。

She was also spending a lot of time on Facebook.

她花了太多时间在脸书上。

It took a lot of time and energy to keep up with everyone's status updates. Catherine started to think.

她花了很多时间与精力去看每个人的状态更新。Catherine 开始思考。

She looked at the list of over 500 friends she had on Facebook and realized some of them were not really friends at all.

看着脸书上 500 多人的好友名单，她明白了有很多人并不是她的真朋友。

Questions 19 to 21 are based on the passage you have just heard.

请根据你刚刚听到的文章回答问题 19 至问题 21。

The answer to Question 21 can be found here for the synonymous sentence: She didn't seem to be doing as well as her Facebook friends.

Question 19: What was one particular convenience Catherine loved about Facebook?

问题 19：Catherine 喜欢脸书的一个尤为突出的便利是什么？

Question 20: How did Catherine feel when her classmates added her as a Facebook friend?

问题 20：当她的同学加她为好友时，Catherine 是怎样的感觉？

Question 21: What made Catherine feel bad about herself later on?

问题 21：为什么 Catherine 后来感觉不开心？

Reading

Text A

Warming-up Activity:

Trust may be the most important factor in successful relationships.

Trust

Andy Rooney

Last night I was driving from Harrisburg to Lewisburg, Pa., a distance of about eighty miles. It was late. I was late and if anyone asked me how fast I was driving, I'd have to plead the Fifth Amendment to avoid self-incrimination. Several times I got stuck behind a slow—moving truck on a narrow road with a solid white line on my left, and I was clinching my fists with impatience.

At one point along an open highway, I came to a crossroads with a traffic light.I was alone on the road by now, but as I approached the light, it turned red and I braked to a halt. I looked left, right and behind me. Nothing. Not a car, no suggestion of headlights, but there I sat, waiting for the light to change, the only human being for at least a mile in any direction.

I started wondering why I refused to run the light. I was not afraid of being arrested, because there was obviously no cop around, and there certainly would have been no danger in going through it.

Much later that night, after I'd met with a group in Lewisburg and had climbed into bed near midnight, the question of why I'd stopped for that light came back to me. I think I stopped because it's part of a contract we all have with each other. It's not only the law, but it's an arrangement we have, and we trust each other to honor it: we don't go through red lights. Like most of us, I'm more apt to be restrained from doing something bad by the social convention that disapproves of it than by any law against it.

It's amazing that we ever trust each other to do the right thing, isn't it？ And we do, too. Trust is our first inclination. We have to make a deliberate decision to mistrust someone or to be suspicious or skeptical. Those attitudes don't come naturally to us.

It's a damn good thing too, because the whole structure of our society depends on mutual trust, not distrust. This whole thing we have going for us would fall apart if we didn't trust each other most of the time.

In Italy, they have an awful time getting any money for the government, because many people just plain don't pay their income tax. Here the Internal

Revenue Service makes some gestures toward enforcing the law, but mostly they just have to trust that we'll pay what we owe.

There has often been talk of a tax revolt in this country, most recently among unemployed auto workers in Michigan, and our government pretty much admits if there was a widespread tax revolt here, they wouldn't be able to do anything about it.

We do what we say we'll do; we show up when we say we'll show up; we deliver when we say we'll deliver; and we pay when we say we'll pay. We trust each other in these matters, and when we don't do what we've promised, it's a deviation from the normal.

It happens often that we don't act in good faith and in a trustworthy manner, but we still consider it unusual, and we're angry or disappointed with the person or organization that violates the trust we have in them. (I'm looking for something good to say about mankind today.)

I hate to see a story about a bank swindler who has jiggered the books. I don't like them, but I trust them. I don't go in and demand that they show me my money all the time just to make sure they still have it.

It's the same buying a can of coffee or a quart of milk. You don't take the coffee home and weigh it to make sure it's a pound. There isn't time in life to distrust every person you meet or every company you do business with.

I hated the company that started selling beer in eleven-ounce bottles years ago. One of the million things we take on trust is that a beer bottle contains twelve ounces.

It's interesting to look around and at people and compare their faith or lack of faith in other people with their success or lack of success in life.

The patsies, the suckers, the people who always assume everyone else is as honest as they are, make out better in the long run than the people who distrust everyone-and they're a lot happier even if they get taken once in a while.

I was so proud of myself for stopping for that red light, and in as much as no one would ever have known what a good person I was on the road from Harrisburg to Lewisburg, I had to tell someone.

Reading Exercises:

1. Why did not the author refuse to run a red light in the absence of anyone?

A. She was afraid of being arrested by the police.

B. She has time so she is not in a hurry.

C. She is mainly bound by social conventions.

D. B and C.

2. Which of the following action does the author approve?

A.Some people always go to the bank to find an operator to confirm their deposit.

B.Bank operators tamper with accounts to defraud their customers' deposits.

C.One company sells only 11 ounces of bottled beer.

D.Someone is very proud of not running a red light.

3. What does the second paragraph from bottom of the article infer?

A. Those who are easily cheated often feel sad.

B. Your trust in others has something to do with your success in life.

C. Those who do not believe in others are unlikely to succeed in life.

D. As long as you are honest and reliable, you will surely succeed in your life.

4. Which of the following statement is Not Correct?

A. Many Italians flagrantly refuse to pay income tax, making it difficult for the government to receive tax.

B. We are always forced to trust others.

C. People's sense of trust does not come naturally.

D. There is no relationship between your trust in others and the success of your life.

5. What is the author's purpose in writing this article?

A.More and more people consciously obey social conventions.

B.Since then, the number of people who run red lights in society has decreased.

C.A and B.

D.After my experience was made public, people were indifferent.

New Words and Phrases

Text A:

plead [pli:d] *v.* ① to state in court that you are guilty or not guilty of a crime（在法

庭）申辩，认罪，辩护 ②to ask sb. for sth. in a very strong and serious way 乞求；恳求 ③ to give sth. as an explanation or excuse for sth. 解释；推说；找借口

phrase: to plead guilty/not guilty 认罪；不认罪

e.g. 1. He advised his client to plead insanity.

他建议他的当事人以精神不正常作为辩护理由。

e.g. 2. One should not plead inexperience in excuse of his mistake.

一个人不应该借口缺乏经验来为他的错误辩解。

clinch [klɪntʃ] *v.* ① secure or fasten by flattening the ends of nails or bolts 钉牢 ② hold in a tight grasp 紧抓；扭住 ③ to succeed in achieving or winning sth. 成功取得；赢得；达成 *n.* a tight or amorous embrace 紧张或多情的拥抱 synonymous: clench

e.g. 1. The boxers clinch and the referee have to separate them.

拳击手扭抱在一起，裁判让他们分开。

e.g. 2. We clinched the agreement with a handshake.

我们握手达成协议。

cop [kɒp] *n.* a police officer 警察 *v.* ① to receive or suffer sth. unpleasant 遭受；忍受 ② to notice sth. 注意到

e.g. 1. There was no question. He looked like a real cop.

毫无疑问，他看上去像个真警察了。

e.g. 2. He copped all the hassle after the accident.

事故发生后，各种罪他都受了。

inclination [ˌɪnklɪˈneɪʃn] *n.* ① a feeling that makes you want to do sth. 倾向；意愿 ② a tendency to do sth. 趋向；趋势

e.g. 1. She lacked any inclination for housework.

她对做家务一点兴趣都没有。

e.g. 2. There is an inclination to treat geography as a less important subject.

人们趋向于把地理当作一门次要的学科。

trustworthy [ˈtrʌstwɜ:ði] *adj.* sb. that you can rely on to be good, honest, sincere, etc. 值得信任的；可信赖的；可靠的 *n.* trustworthiness

e.g. He is a trustworthy and level-headed leader.

他是个头脑冷静、值得信赖的领导。

apt to likely or having a natural tendency to do sth. 易于…… ；有……倾向

e.g. Babies are apt to put objects into their mouths.

婴儿爱把东西往嘴里塞。

fall apart ① to be in very bad condition so that parts are breaking off 破碎；破裂 ② to have so many problems that it is no longer possible to exist or function 破裂；崩溃

e.g. 1. His promising career began to fall apart.

他那本来前程似锦的职业生涯开始崩塌了。

e.g. 2. Their marriage finally fell apart.

他们的婚姻终于破裂了。

pretty much almost; almost completely 几乎；差不多

e.g. One dog looks pretty much like another to me.

在我看来，狗长得都差不多。

deviation from 脱离；逸出；与 …… 不符合

e.g. Any deviation from the party's faith is seen as betrayal.

任何背离党的信仰的行为都被视作背叛。

restrain from 抑制；制止；阻止……去……

e.g. She managed to restrain him from taking such a foolish step.

她设法阻止了他走这么愚蠢的一步。

Text B

Warming-up Activity:

The Kite Runner is an inspiring novel about a Pashtun named Amir who looks back on his life during his transition from childhood into adulthood. Amir grew up in a rich district of Kabul, Afghanistan. His father was a respected man, but Amir struggled to live up to his father's standards. Ali and his son Hassan (Amir's best friend), are both loyal servants to Baba and Amir. Amir and Hassan's relationship was forever changed when they took part in an annual kite-fighting tournament. Their fates reflect the eventual tragedy of the world around them. This book is also concerned with friendship, betrayal and redemption, with the bonds between fathers and sons—their love, their sacrifices and their lives.

The Kite Runner (Excerpt)

—Khaled Hosseini

Usually, each neighborhood held its own competition. But that year, the tournament was going to be held in my neighborhood, Wazir Akbar Khan, and several other districts—Karteh-Char, Karteh-Parwan, Mekro-Rayan, and Koteh-Sangi—had been invited. You could hardly go anywhere without hearing talk of the upcoming tournament. Word had it this was going to be the biggest tournament in twenty-five years.

One night that winter, with the big contest only four days away, Baba and I sat in his study in overstuffed leather chairs by the glow of the fireplace. We were sipping tea, talking. Ali had served dinner earlier—potatoes and curried cauliflower over rice—and had retired for the night with Hassan. Baba was fattening his pipe and I was asking him to tell the story about the winter a pack of wolves had descended from the mountains in Herat and forced everyone to stay indoors for a week, when he lit a match and said, casually, "I think maybe you'll win the tournament this year. What do you think?"

I didn't know what to think. Or what to say. Was that what it would take? Had he just slipped me a key? I was a good kite fighter. Actually, a very good one. A few times, I'd even come close to winning the winter tournament-once, I'd made it to the final three. But coming close wasn't the same as winning, was it? Baba hadn't "come close". He had won because winners won and everyone else just went Home. Baba was used to winning, winning at everything he set his mind to. Didn't he have a right to expect the same from his son? And just imagine. If I did win...

Baba smoked his pipe and talked. I pretended to listen. But I couldn't listen, not really, because Baba's casual little comment had planted a seed in my head: the resolution that I would win that winter's tournament. I was going to win. There was no other viable option. I was going to win, and I was going to run that last kite. Then I'd bring it home and show it to Baba. Show him once and for all that his son was worthy. Then maybe my life as a ghost in this house would finally be over. I let myself dream: I imagined conversation and laughter over dinner instead of silence broken only by the clinking of silverware and the occasional grunt. I envisioned us taking a Friday drive in Baba's car to Paghman, stopping on the way at Ghargha Lake for some fried trout and potatoes. We'd go to the zoo to see Marjan the lion, and maybe Baba wouldn't yawn and steal looks at his wristwatch all the time. Maybe Baba would even read one of my stories. I'd write him a hundred if I thought he'd read one. Maybe he'd call me Amir jan like Rahim Khan did. And maybe, just maybe, I would finally be pardoned for killing my mother.

Baba was telling me about the time he'd cut fourteen kites on the same day. I smiled, nodded, laughed at all the right places, but I hardly heard a word he said. I had a mission now. And I wasn't going to fail Baba. Not this time.

It snowed heavily the night before the tournament. Hassan and I sat under the kursi and played panjpar as wind-rattled tree branches tapped on the window. Earlier that day, I'd asked Ali to set up the kursi for us - which was basically an electric heater under a low table covered with a thick, quilted blanket. Around the table, he arranged mattresses and cushions, so as many as twenty people could sit and slip their legs under. Hassan and I used to spend entire snowy days snug under the kursi, playing chess, cards - mostly panjpar.

I killed Hassan's ten of diamonds, played him two jacks and a six. Next door, in Baba's study, Baba and Rahim Khan were discussing Business with a couple of other men - one of them I recognized as Assef's father. Through the wall, I could hear the scratchy sound of Radio Kabul News.

Hassan killed the six and picked up the jacks. On the radio, Daoud Khan was announcing something about foreign investments.

"He says someday we'll have television in Kabul." I said.

"Who?"

"Daoud Khan, you ass, the president."

Hassan giggled. "I heard they already have it in Iran." he said.

I sighed. "Those Iranians..." For a lot of Hazaras, Iran represented a sanctuary of sorts-I guess because, like Hazaras, most Iranians were Shi'a Muslims. But I remembered something my teacher had said that summer about Iranians, that they were grinning smooth talkers who patted you on the back with one hand and picked your pocket with the other. I told Baba about that and he said my teacher was one of those jealous Afghans, jealous because Iran was a rising power in Asia and most people around the world couldn't even find Afghanistan on a world map. "It hurts to say that." he said, shrugging. "But better to get hurt by the truth than comforted with a lie."

"I'll buy you one someday." I said.

Hassan's face brightened. "A television? In truth?"

"Sure. And not the black-and-white kind either. We'll probably be grown-ups by then, but I'll get us two. One for you and one for me."

"I'll put it on my table, where I keep my drawings." Hassan said.

Reading Exercises:

Check whether each statement is true (T) or false (F).

1. Amir has a misson to win the first prize in the upcoming tournament for being forgiven by his father.

2. Amir had won the winter tournament for a few times and had made it to the final three only once .
3. It is usual for the family member that taking a Friday drive in Baba's car and stopping on the way at Ghargha Lake for some fried trout and potatoes.
4. Rahim Khan is as close as a family to Amir who has read one of the stories Amir writes.
5. Amir promised that he would buy Hassana a television when they grow up.

New Words and Phrases

Text B:

retrieve [rɪˈtriːv] *v.* ① to bring or get sth. back, especially from a place where it should not be 取回；索回 ② to make a bad situation better; to get back sth. that was lost 扭转颓势；挽回；找回

e.g. 1. The police have managed to retrieve some of the stolen money.

警方已经追回了部分被盗钱款。

e.g. 2. You can only retrieve the situation by apologizing.

你只有道歉才能挽回这个局面。

cowardly [ˈkaʊədlɪ] *adj.* lacking courage; ignobly timid and faint-hearted 怯懦的；胆小的；懦弱的；*adv.* 怯懦地；胆怯地；*n.* coward 胆小鬼；懦夫；胆怯者

e.g. 1. He was weak, cowardly and treacherous.

他软弱，胆怯，奸诈。

e.g. 2. When I was a boy, I was too cowardly to go out at night.

当我还是个小孩时，我胆小得晚上不敢出门。

silverware [ˈsɪlvəweə(r)] *n.* ① a silver cup that you win in a sports competition（体育比赛中的）银杯 ② objects that are made of or covered with silver, especially knives, forks, dishes, etc. that are used for eating and serving food 银器，镀银器皿（尤指餐具）

e.g. 1. Everton paraded their recently acquired silverware.

埃弗顿展示了他们最近获得的银杯。

e.g. 2. Her silverware consists of knives, forks, spoons, a water pitcher, and candlesticks.

她所有的银器包括刀、叉、匙、一个水壶，还有烛台。

envision [ɪnˈvɪʒn] *v.* to imagine what a situation will be like in the future, especially a situation you intend to work towards 设想；想象；预想

e.g. 1. They envision an equal society, free of poverty and disease.

他们向往一个没有贫穷和疾病的平等社会。

e.g. 2. It's not documented in history, but it's not hard to envision.

历史上并没有记载，但不难想象。

sanctuary [ˈsæŋktʃuəri] *n.* ① a holy building or the part of it that is considered the most holy 圣所；圣殿 ② a safe place, especially one where people who are being chased or attacked can stay and be protected 避难所；庇护所

e.g. Am I actually being invited into the sanctuary?

难道我真的被邀请到这间圣殿里来了？

look back on to think about sth. in your past 回首（往事）；回忆；回顾

e.g. Now I can look back on the whole tragedy from a distance of forty years.

时隔 40 年后，现在我可以回顾整个悲剧了。

live up to to do as well as or be as good as other people expect you to 达到，符合，不辜负（他人的期望）

e.g. She tries up to live up to her ideals.

她努力去实现她的理想。

have a right 有资格……；有权利……

e.g. They have a right to be mad. We all have a right to be mad, and we have a right to say whatever.

他们有权利生气。我们都有权利生气，我们也有权利畅所欲言。

descend from 起源于；由……传下来的

e.g. These ideas descend from those of the ancient philosophers.

这些观点来源于那些古代哲学家的思想。

tap on 轻轻敲击（某物的表面），轻击……（某部位）

e.g. Hmm, tapping on your desk like this can be so annoying.

嗯，敲桌子真的很烦人。

Writing

Part 1 命题分析

信函写作

1. 定义

信函写作是指用书面的形式向亲人、朋友、同事问候、谈话、联系事宜，它具有明确而特定的用途和接受对象，并有固定的或惯用的格式。

2. 写作步骤

基本结构：第一段直击问题，用“一句话”来具体展现和说明。第二、三段为对问题产生的原因或解决方法的分析，为文章的主体段落，要注意分层展开。

第一步：写信原因或目的、引出话题。

第二步：阐述话题，明确观点。

第三步：总结话题，表达祝愿。

3. 信函写作模板

信函写作按照开头段、正文段和结尾段三个部分呈现，供同学们研究、模仿，以便快速提高此类作文的写作水平。

开头段：

a. I would like to thank you from the bottom of my heart for…

b. Words fail to convey my gratitude to you.

c. It is a pleasure for me to invite you on behalf of … to accept …

d. Thanks so much for your letter , which arrived …

e. I am writing to you with reference to.../in connection with …

f. I am writing to express my sincere gratitude for…

g. I would be grateful if you could / would …

h. It will be appreciated if you can / could …

i. I would like to know some information on …

j. I was truly enraptured beyond expression to…

正文段：

A. 感谢信

I'd like you to know how much your...meant to me. You have a positive genius for....I not only enjoyed..., but also.... I shall ever remember...as one of the most...in my life. I hope to have the opportunity of reciprocating. Would you kindly let me know...? I will feel very honored and pleased if you are available to....

B. 申请信

I feel I am competent to meet the requirements you have listed. On the one hand, ... On the other hand, ... I am enclosing my resume for your kind consideration and reference.I shall be much obliged if you will offer me a precious opportunity to an interview.

C. 道歉信

There are four main reasons why I.... To begin with, ... Under that circumstance.... Therefore, it was not my power to.... Moreover, ... What's more.... Finally,.... If possible, I would like to suggest that.... I shall be obliged if you will kindly write and tell me....

D. 投诉信

The focus of the complaint is.... For one thing, ... For another, ... Under these circumstances, I found /find it.... Honestly speaking, ... In addition, ... All in all, there is still much room for improvement. I do hope....

E. 拒绝信

This has been a tough decision for me, but I have to.... On the one hand, ... On the other hand, ... In view of these, I regret that.... I sincerely hope this does not bring you much inconvenience. I feel very sorry to disappoint you. If, ... I will.... I do appreciate your.... Meanwhile, I wish....

F. 祝贺信

I have just learned that.... I hasten to tender you a word of congratulations on this splendid success of.... It is indeed a remarkable thing for.... The success of your... proves not only..., but also....

结尾段：

a. Your prompt and favorable attention to...would be highly appreciated.

b. I would like to thank you for your generous help in....

c. I shall be much obliged to you if you.... Thanks for your kind consideration and I look forward to receiving your earliest reply.

d. I will greatly appreciate a response from you at your earliest convenience.

e. I am looking forward to your replies at your earliest convenience.

f. Again, please accept my warm... and please give my best wishes to....

g. Thanks for your time and kind consideration. Best regards for your health and success.

Part 2 练习

Directions: *For this part, you are allowed 30 minutes to write a letter to decline an offer with your reasons. You should write at least 120 words but no more than 180 words.*

【审题】：李萍同学去一家翻译公司面试，她清楚地认识到自己缺乏英语专业能力并且更倾向于程序设计方面的工作岗位，她需要写一封回绝信。

【中心思想】：婉拒工作职位。

【写作提纲】：（1）对公司提供职位表示感谢；

（2）解释为何不能接受职位；

（3）表达对公司的良好祝愿。

【范文】

Dear Sir/Madam,

I am responding to your job offer on December 20, 2018. I was informed that I would be offered the position as an interpreter for your company. I cordially appreciate your trust and I am much obliged to you for providing me with this valuable opportunity.

However, I have to tell you that I cannot accept it. The major reason is that I don’t think I am the most appropriate candidate for this post. As an non-English major, though my written and spoken English are outstanding than most of my peers, I’m not well trained in translation, not to mention interpretation, which, I believe is highly demanding. Maybe my performance in the oral examination has misled you. Actually, I'm more interested and more competent in my own major, that is, program designing. Last but not the least, I 've got an offer from another company.

Nevertheless, I, again, want to express my sincere gratefulness and I earnestly apologize for any inconvenience hereby caused. Finally, I hope you can find the ideal candidate as soon as possible.

Yours sincerely,

Li Ping

Vocabulary Exercises

A. *Fill in the blanks with the words in the box. Read the sentences carefully before making your choices. You may not use any of the words in the bank more than once. Change the form where necessary.*

cop sanctuary plead retrieve cowardly clinch trustworthy envision silverware inclination

1. Willingham insisted on his innocence, refusing to _______ guilty even to avoid execution.
2. Mike Bryan talked about getting the chance to _______ the victory.
3. Frank didn't like having the ________ know where to find him.
4. You must follow your own ________ when choosing a career.
5. He wanted to find someone who was ______ , responsible, and extremely honest.
6. The men were trying to ________ weapons left when the army abandoned the island.
7. His ________ behavior was laughed at by his colleagues.
8. There was a serving spoon missing when Nina put the ________ back in its box.
9. We ________ a federation of companies in the future.
10. The church became a ________ for the refugees.

B. *Fill in the blanks with the phrases in the box. Read the sentences carefully before* *making your choices. You may not use any of the phrases in the bank more than once. Change the form where necessary.*

fall apart	tap on	deviation from	restrain from	look back on	descend from
live up to	have a right	pretty much	apt to		

1. This type of weather is ___________ be more common in winter.
2. She ___________ completely when her only child died.
3. He'd do ___________ anything on a dare.
4. ___________ the norm is not tolerated.
5. They like to ___________ those unforgettable years in the army.
6. He failed to ___________ his parents' expectations.
7. People ___________ to live, a right not to be killed.
8. Our prejudice must ___________ the female branch.
9. Chinese English student must ___________ using the Chinese-English translation thinking process that he is accustomed to.
10. I felt this ___________ my shoulder, and I turned around to see this giant girl in a hoodie sweatshirt emerge from the crowd.

Extended Exercises

Cloze

There is a passage with 10 blanks. You are required to select one word for each blank from a list of choices in a word bank following the passage. Read the passage through carefully before making your choices. Each choice in the bank is identified by a letter.

A) cautiously	B) commit	C) control	D) cycling
E) effectively	F) increased	G) involved	H) limited
I) phenomenon	J) preventing	K) sensitive	L) slowing
M) solution	N) sufficient	O) vigorous	

As if you needed another reason to hate the gym, it now turns out that exercise can exhaust not only your muscles, but also your eyes. Fear not, however, for coffee can stimulate them again. During ___1___ exercise, our muscles tire as they run out of fuel and build up waste products. Muscle performance can also be affected by a ___2___ called "central fatigue", in which an imbalance in the body's chemical messengers prevents the central nervous system from directing muscle movements ___3___. It was not known, however, whether central fatigue might also affect motor systems not directly ___4___ in the exercise itself, such as those that move the eyes. To find out, researchers gave 11 volunteer cyclists a carbohydrate（碳水化合物的）___5___ either with a moderate dose of caffeine（咖啡因）, which is known to stimulate the central nervous system, or as a placebo（安慰剂）without, during 3 hours of ___6___. After exercising, the scientists tested the cyclists with eye-tracking cameras to see how well their brains could still ___7___ their visual system. The team found that exercise reduced the speed of rapid eye movements by about 8%, ___8___ their ability to capture new visual information. The caffeine, the equivalent of two strong cups of coffee, was ___9___ to reverse this effect, with some cyclists even displaying ___10___ eye movement speeds. So it might be a good idea to get someone else to drive you home after that marathon.

Paragraph Matching

You are going to read a passage with ten statements attached to it. Each statement contains information given in one of the paragraphs. Identify the paragraph from which the information is derived. You may choose a paragraph more than once. Each paragraph is marked with a letter.

Team Spirit

[A] Teams have become the basic building blocks of organizations. Recruitment advertisements routinely call for "team players". Business schools grade their students in part on their performance in group projects. Office managers knock down walls to encourage team building. Teams are as old as civilization, of course: even Jesus had 12 co-workers. But a new report by Deloitte, "Global Human Capital Trends", based on a survey of more than 7000 executives in over 130 countries, suggests that the fashion for teamwork has reached a new high. Almost half of those surveyed said their companies were either in the middle of restructuring or about to embark on（开始）it; and for the most part, restructuring meant putting more emphasis on teams.

[B] Companies are abandoning conventional functional departments and organising employees into cross- disciplinary teams that focus on particular products, problems or customers. These teams are gaining more power to run their own affairs. They are also spending more time working with each other rather than reporting upwards. Deloitte argues that a new organisational form is on the rise: a network of teams is replacing the conventional hierarchy（等级体制）.

[C] The fashion for teams is driven by a sense that the old way of organising people is too rigid for both the modern marketplace and the expectations of employees. Technological innovation places greater value on agility（灵活性）. John Chambers, chairman of Cisco Systems Inc., a worldwide leader in electronics products, says that "we compete against market transitions（过渡）, not competitors. Product transitions used to take five or seven years; now they take one or two." Digital technology also makes it easier for people to co-ordinate their activities without resorting to hierarchy. The "millennials"（千禧一代）who will soon make up half the workforce in rich countries were raised from nursery school onwards to work in groups.

[D] The fashion for teams is also spreading from the usual corporate suspects (such as GE and IBM) to some more unusual ones. The Cleveland Clinic, a hospital operator, has reorganised its medical staff into teams to focus on particular treatment areas; consultants, nurses and others collaborate closely instead of being separated by speciality（专业）and rank. The US Army has gone the same way. In his book, Team of Teams, General Stanley McChrystal describes how the army's hierarchical structure hindered its operations during the early stages of the Iraq war. His solution was to learn something from the rebels it was fighting: decentralising authority to self-organising teams.

[E] A good rule of thumb is that as soon as generals and hospital administrators jump on a management bandwagon（追随一种管理潮流）, it is time to ask questions. Leigh Thompson of Kellogg School of Management in Illinois warns that, "Teams are not always the answer—teams may provide insight, creativity and knowledge in a way that a person working independently cannot; but teamwork may also lead to confusion, delay and poor decision-making. "The late Richard Hackman of Harvard University once argued, "I have no question that when you have a team, the possibility exists that it will generate magic, producing something extraordinary .... But don't count on it."

[F] Hackman (who died in 2013) noted that teams are hindered by problems of co-ordination and motivation that chip away at the benefits of collaboration. High-flyers（能干的人）who are forced to work in teams may be undervalued and free-riders empowered. Group-think may be unavoidable. In a study of 120 teams of senior executives, he discovered that less than 10% of their supposed members agreed on who exactly was on the team. If it is hard enough to define a team's membership, agreeing on its purpose is harder still.

[G] Profound changes in the workforce are making teams trickier to manage. Teams work best if their members have a strong common culture. This is hard to achieve when, as is now the case in many big firms, a large proportion of staff are temporary contractors. Teamwork improves with time: America's National Transportation Safety Board found that 73% of the incidents in its civil-aviation database occurred on a crew's first day of flying together. However, as Amy Edmondson of Harvard points out, organisations increasingly use "team" as a verb rather than a noun: they form teams for specific purposes and then quickly disband them.

[H] The least that can be concluded from this research is that companies need to think harder about managing teams. They need to rid their minds of sentimentalism（感情用事）: the most successful teams have leaders who are able to set an overall direction and take immediate action. They need to keep teams small and focused: giving in to pressure to be more "inclusive" is a guarantee of dysfunction. Jeff Bezos, Amazon's boss, says that "If I see more than two pizzas for lunch, the team is too big." They need to immunise teams against group-think: Hackman argued that the best ones contain "deviant"（离经叛道者）

who are willing to do something that may be upsetting to others.

[I] A new study of 12000 workers in 17 countries by Steelcase, a furniture-maker which also does consulting, finds that the best way to ensure employees are "engaged" is to give them more control over where and how they do their work—which may mean liberating them from having to do everything in collaboration with others.

[J] However, organisations need to learn something bigger than how to manage teams better: they need to be in the habit of asking themselves whether teams are the best tools for the job. Team-building skills are in short supply: Deloitte reports that only 12% of the executives they contacted feel they understand the way people work together in networks and only 21% feel confident in their ability to build cross-functional teams. Loosely managed teams can become hotbeds of distraction-employees routinely complain that they can't get their work done because they are forced to spend too much time in meetings or compelled to work in noisy offices. Even in the age of open - plan offices and social networks some work is best left to the individual.

1. Successful team leaders know exactly where the team should go and are able to take prompt action.
2. Decentralisation of authority was also found to be more effective in military operations.
3. In many companies, the conventional form of organisation is giving way to a network of teams.
4. Members of poorly managed teams are easily distracted from their work.
5. Teamwork is most effective when team members share the same culture.
6. According to a report by Deloitte, teamwork is becoming increasingly popular among companies.
7. Some team members find it hard to agree on questions like membership and the team's purpose.
8. Some scholars think teamwork may not always be reliable, despite its potential to work wonders.

9. To ensure employees' commitment, it is advisable to give them more flexibility as to where and how they work.
10. Product transitions take much less time now than in the past.

Cultural Translation

Directions: *For this part, you are allowed 30 minutes to translate a passage from Chinese into English.*

长江是亚洲最长、世界上第三长的河流。长江流经多种不同的生态系统，是诸多濒危物种的栖息地，灌溉了中国五分之一的土地。长江流域（river basin）居住着中国三分之一的人口。长江在中国历史、文化和经济上起着很大的作用。长江三角洲（delta）产出多达 20% 的中国国民生产总值。几千年来，长江一直被用于供水、运输和工业生产。长江上还坐落着世界最大的水电站。

练习答案

Reading Exercises

Text A: 1 ～ 5 CDBAC

Text B: 1 ～ 5 TFFFT

Vocabulary Exercises

A:

1. plead
2. clinch
3. cops
4. inclinations
5. trustworthy
6. retrieve
7. cowardly
8. silverware
9. envision
10. sanctuary

B:

1. apt to
2. fell apart
3. pretty much
4. Deviation from
5. look back on
6. live up to
7. have a right
8. descend from
9. restrain from
10. tap on

Extended Exercises

Cloze:

1 ～ 10: OIEGM DCJNF

Paragraph Matching:

1 ～ 10: HDBJG AFEIC

Cultural Translation:

The Yangtze River is the longest in Asia and the third longest in the world. The river, which flows through varied ecosystems along its passage, offers habitats for many endangered species and provides irrigation for 1/5 of China's land. The Yangtze River basin is home to 1/3 of China's population. The river plays a very important role in China historically, culturally and economically. The Yangtze River Delta contributes up to 20% of China's GDP. For millennia, the Yangtze River has been used for water supply, shipment and industrial activities. The world's largest hydropower station is also built on the river.

Unit 7 Modern Technology

Learning Objectives

After completing this unit, you will be able to do the following:

◇ Practice for the skill: How to conclude the Main Idea;

◇ Grasp the main idea and the structure of the texts;

◇ Master the key language points and grammatical structure in the text;

◇ Conduct a series of reading, speaking and writing activities related to the theme in the unit.

Learning Difficult Points

In this unit, you will learn some difficult points listed below.

◇ Listening: How to conclude the Main Idea.

◇ Writing: Applied Writing

Outline

The Following are the main sections in this Unit.

1. Listening
2. Speaking
3. Reading: Text A & Text B
4. Writing
5. Extended Exercises

Vocabulary

Listed below are some words appearing in this unit that you should make part of your vocabulary.

misguided
scenario
premise
dictate
interact

Looking Ahead

Modern Technology

Science and Technology play an increasingly important role in modern society and life.

Without Moern Science and Technology, it is impossible to build Modern Agriculture, Modern Industry or Modern National Defence.

Introduction

The ties that bind the world's two biggest economies are unravelling, in fits and starts. On December 31st 2020, the New York Stock Exchange (NYSE) announced that it would delist China Telecom, China Mobile and China Unicom, three telecoms giants, shares in which have been traded on Wall Street for years. This set off a fit among their American shareholders. As the trio's share prices swung wildly, funds scrambled to sell their stakes before the delisting. Then came the start.

Late on January 4th the NYSE declared it would not eject the firms after all. Those same funds faced the prospect of repurchasing the shares, the price of which had popped up on news of the NYSE's U-turn. If that weren't chaotic enough, two days later the NYSE changed its mind again. It would, after all, boot out the three companies.

One thing is clear: Chinese companies listed in America face uncertain times. In December Mr Trump signed a bipartisan law that would expel from exchanges in America those companies that do not allow American regulators to audit their accounts, which is the case for many Chinese ones. On top of this law, Mr Trump's executive order is likely to remain a problem; Joe Biden may hesitate to rescind it after he takes office on January 20th. It affects more than 30 firms deemed too cosy with the PLA. To comply, FTSE Russell, which maintains global equity indices, plans to cut at least 11 Chinese technology firms from its roster.

(Excerpted from *The Economist*)

Speaking

Consider the following questions before reading:

1. Please discuss how to interest a sponsor.
2. What will an enterprise obtain if it wants to sponsor an exhibition?

Conversation

Role-play: ask someone to raise sponsorship for a technical exhibition. Talk about the importance of an international exhibition.

A: Glad to meet you, Mr. Smith. I'm Xie Li, organizer of the exhibition.

B: It's my pleasure to meet you.

A: I'm here to discuss with you about sponsoring the exhibition.

B: Happy to be of any help to you. What exhibition is it?

A: The 10th China (Shenzhen) International Battery Exhibition. The attendees are top companies across the world.

B: And when do you plan to hold the exhibition?

A: It'll be subject to the changing market. We shall conduct a survey to find out if there will be exhibitions of a similar kind. You know, there must be an interval of 3 ~ 6 months. As for the exact dates, we'll do our best to give you a reply as soon as possible.

B: As a final point, can we become the agency of the battery?

A: No problem. But you will have to sponsor with a considerable amount of money then. Further information about terms and conditions are stated in the draft contract.

B: Thank you. We have to give serious consideration to the contract. We'll let you know by fax once we've decided.

A. Thank you for coming. We look forward to seeing you soon again.

UNIT 7 Modern Technology

Listening

Listening skills are fundamental to success in English Listening. Through this part, we will have a detailed introduction to promote listening efficiency we could enhance by analyzing the three parts—News, Long conversation and Passage.

Listening Skills for Passage (3)

Keys to conclude the main idea:

In listening comprehension, concluding the main idea is one of the emphases in various English tests. Questions relvevant with main idea include: What is the main idea of the passage? /What is the passage mainly about? /What is the best title for the passage? / What is the speaker talking about? / What is the author mainly discussing? and so on.

To get the main idea of a passage is essential for listening comprehension. First, try to get the topic sentence in a passage. The topic sentence usually appears at the very beginning to briefly introduce the passage or at the end to summarize the main idea. Second, try to find out the key words in provided choices. E.g., repeated words in each item; specific details concerning people, time, place, number, reason, etc. Last but not least, infer the main idea logically from the clues.

Example（出自四级听力原文）

The massive decline in sleep happened so

slowly and quietly that few seemed to notice the trend. Was it because of the growing attraction of the Internet, video games and endless TV channels? Never disconnecting from work? No matter how it happened, millions of Americans are putting their health, quality of life and even length of life in danger.

睡眠时间的大幅减少发生得如此缓慢和安静，以至于似乎很少有人注意到这一趋势。是因为互联网、电子游戏和看不完的电视频道越来越吸引人吗？仍然在工作？不管这是怎么发生的，数以百万计的美国人正在把他们的健康、生活质量甚至寿命都置于危险之中。

短文开头简明扼要地综述了大量美国人睡眠不足现象。并指出了睡眠不足对健康、生活质量，甚至寿命的危害。

New evidence shows why getting enough sleep is a top priority. Some 40% of Americans get less than 7 hours of shut-eye on week nights. "The link between sleep and health, and bad sleep and disease is becoming clearer and clearer." says Lawrence Alberstaine, a sleep expert at Harvard University. For example, sleep duration has declined from some 8 hours in the 1950s to 7 in recent years. At the same time, high blood pressure has become an increasing problem. Blood pressure and heart rate are typically at their lowest levels during sleep. People who sleep less tend to have higher blood pressure, heart attack, diabetes, weight gain and other problems.

新的证据证明了充足睡眠至关重要。大约 40% 的美国人每周晚上的平均睡眠时间少于 7 小时。哈佛大学睡眠专家劳伦斯 · 阿尔

接着，短文介绍了充足睡眠的重要性。睡眠不足易于造成健康问题。

伯斯坦 (Lawrence Alberstaine) 说：“睡眠与健康之间的联系，以及睡眠障碍与疾病之间的联系正变得越来越清晰。”例如，睡眠时间从20世纪50年代的8小时左右下降到近年来的7小时。与此同时，高血压已成为一个日益严重的问题。人在睡眠时，其血压和心率通常处于最低水平。睡眠不足的人易于有高血压、心脏病、糖尿病、体重增加等问题。

Sleeping better may help fight off illness. “When people are sleep-deprived, there are higher levels of stress hormones in their bodies which can decrease immune function.” says Doctor Felice, of Northwestern University in Chicago. A university of Chicago study shows people who sleep well live longer. So say good night sooner and it may help you stay active and vital to a ripe old age.

短文在结尾指出，睡眠好的人更长寿，呼吁大家重视充足睡眠的重要性。

良好的睡眠有助于抵抗疾病。芝加哥西北大学的费利斯博士说：“人在睡眠不足时，体内的压力激素水平较高，这会降低免疫功能。”芝加哥大学的一项研究表明，睡眠好的人更长寿。所以早点说晚安，这可能会帮助你在晚年保持健康与活力。

Q1. What is the speaker mainly talking about?

Q2. What do we learn from the talk about today’s Americans?

Q3. What does the speaker say will happen to people who lack sleep?

第一题考查短文的主旨，通过题干中反复出现的 sleep，及短文开头、结尾内容的呼应，不难得出答案为 A。

Question 1:

A) The importance of sleep to a healthy life.

B) Reasons for Americans' decline in sleep.

C) Some tips to improve the quality of sleep.

D) Diseases associated with lack of sleep.

Question 2:

A) They are more health-conscious.

B) They are changing their living habits.

C) They get less and less sleep.

D) They know the dangers of lack of sleep.

Question 3:

A) Their weight will go down.

B) Their mind function will deteriorate.

C) Their work efficiency will decrease.

D) Their blood pressure will rise.

Reading

Text A

Warming-up Activity:

Jeffrey D Sachs, professor of sustainable development and professor of health policy and management at Columbia University, is director of Columbia's Center for Sustainable Development and the UN Sustainable Development Solutions Network.

America's Misguided War on Chinese Technology

By Jeffrey D Sachs

The worst foreign-policy decision by the United States of the last generation —and perhaps longer—was the "war of choice" that it launched in lraq in 2003 for the stated purpose of eliminating weapons of mass destruction that did not, in fact, exist. Understanding the illogic behind that disastrous decision has never been more relevant, because it is being used to justify a similarly misguided US policy today.

The decision to invade Iraq followed the illogic of then—US vice—president Richard Cheney, who declared that even if the risk of WMD falling into terrorist hands was tiny—Say, 1% — we should act as if that scenario would certainly occur.

Such reasoning is guaranteed to lead to wrong decisions more often than not. Yet the US and some of its allies are now using the Cheney Doctrine to attack Chinese technology. The US government argues that because we can't know with certainty that Chinese technologies are safe, we should act as if they are certainly dangerous and bar them.

Proper decision-making applies probability estimates to alternative actions. A generation ago, US policymakers should have considered not only the (alleged) 1% risk of WMD falling into terrorist hands, but also the 99% risk of a war based on flawed premises. By focusing only on the 1% risk, Cheney (and many others) distracted the public's attention from the much greater likelihood that the Iraq war lacked justification and that it would gravely destabilize the Middle East and global politics.

The problem with the Cheney Doctrine is not only that it dictates taking actions predicated on small risks without considering the potentially very high costs. Politicians are tempted to whip up fears for ulterior purposes.

That is what US leaders are doing again: creating a panic over Chinese technology companies by raising, and exaggerating, tiny risks. The most pertinent case (but not the only one) is the US government attack on the wireless broadband company Huawei. The US is closing its markets to the company and trying hard to shut down its business around the world. As with Iraq, the US could end up creating a geopolitical disaster for no reason.

I have followed Huawei's technological advances and work in developing countries, as I believe that fifth-generation (5G) and other digital technologies offer a huge boost to ending poverty and other Sustainable Development Goals. I have similarly interacted with other telecom companies and encouraged the industry to set up actions for the United Nations' SDGs. When I wrote a short foreword (without compensation) for a Huawei report on the topic, and was criticized by foes of China, I asked top industry and government officials for evidence of wayward activities by Huawei. I heard repeatedly that Huawei behaves no differently than trusted industry leaders.

The US government nonetheless argues that Huawei's 5G equipment could undermine global security. A "back door" in Huawei's software or hardware, US officials claim, could enable the Chinese government to engage in surveillance around the world. After all, US officials note, China's laws require Chinese companies to cooperate with the government for purposes of national security.

Now, the facts are these. Huawei's 5G equipment is low-cost and high-quality, currently ahead of many competitors, and already rolling out. Its high-performance results from years of substantial spending on research and development, scale economies, and learning by doing in the Chinese digital marketplace. Given the technology 's importance for their sustainabe development, low-income economies around the world would be foolhardy to reject an early 5G rollout.

Yet despite providing no evidence of back doors, the US is telling the world to stay away from Huawei. The US claims are generic. As a US Federal Communications Commissioner put it, "The country that owns 5G will own innovations and set the standards for the rest of the world, and that country is currently not likely to be the United States." Other countries, most notably the United Kingdom, have found no back doors in Huawei's hardware and software. Even if back doors were discovered later, they could almost surely be closed at that point.

The debate over Huawei rages in Germany, where the US government threatens to curtail intelligence cooperation unless the authorities exclude Huawei's 5G technology. Perhaps as a result of the US pressure, Germany's spy chief recently made a claim tantamount to the Cheney Doctrine. "Infrastructure is not a suitable area for a group that cannot be trusted fully." He offered no evidence of specific misdeeds. Chancellor Angela Merkel, by contrast, is fighting behind the scenes to leave the market open for Huawei.

Ironically, though predictably, the US complaints partly reflect America's own surveillance activities at home and abroad. Chinese equipment might make secret surveillance by the US government more difficult. But unwarranted surveillance by any government should be ended. Independent UN monitoring to curtail such activities should become part of the global telecommunications system. In short, we should choose diplomacy and institutional safeguards, not a technology war.

The threat of US demands to blockade Huawei concerns more than the early rollout of the 5G network. The risks to the rules-based trading system are profound. Now that the US is no longer the world's undisputed technology leader, President Donald Trump and his advisers don't want to compete according to a rules-based system. Their goal is to contain China's technological rise. Their simultaneous attempt to neutralize the World Trade Organization by disabling its dispute settlement system shows the same disdain for global rules.

If the Trump administration "succeeds" in dividing the world into separate technology camps, the risks of future conflicts will multiply. The US championed open trade after World War II not only to boost global efficiency and expand markets for American technology, but also to reverse the collapse of international trade in the 1930s. That collapse stemmed in part from protectionist tariffs imposed by the US under the 1930 Smoot-Hawley Act, which amplified the Great Depression, in turn contributing to the rise of Adolf Hitler and, ultimately, the outbreak of World War II.

In international affairs, no less than in other domains, stoking fears and acting on them, rather than on the evidence, is the path to ruin. Let's stick to rationality, evidence and rules as the safest course of action. And let us create independent monitors to curtail the threat of any country using global networks for surveillance of or cyberwarfare on others. That way, the world can get on with the urgent task of harnessing breakthrough digital technologies for the global good.

Reading Exercises:

1. Which of the following items concerned with American decision to invade Iraq is not mentioned in the passage?

A. It is expected to eliminate weapons of mass destruction.

B. Richard Cheney declared that the risk of WMD falling into terrorist hands was 99%.

C. The disastrous decision has stated purpose.

D. The worst foreign-policy decision by the United States of the last generation – was the "war of choice" that it launched in 2003.

2. Which of the following statement is Not the author's view?

A. He believes that fifth-generation (5G) and other digital technologies offer a huge boost to ending poverty and other Sustainable Development Goals.

B. Huawei's 5G equipment is high-cost and high-quality, currently ahead of many competitors, and already rolling out.

C. That is what US leaders are doing again: creating a panic over Chinese technology companies by raising, and exaggerating, tiny risks.

D. The most relevant case (but not the only one) is the US government's attack on the Wireless broadband company Huawei.

3. As with Iraq, the US could end up creating a geopolitical disaster <u>for no reason</u>. The underlined phrase means _______.

A.bottomless

B.with reason

C.baselessly

D.ceaselessly

4. Which of the following words can substitute for the word "disdain" in "the same disdain for global rules"?

A. respect

B. contempt

C. praise

D. shame

5. Chancellor Angela Merkel's attitude towards Huawei's market share in German is________.

A. negative

B. critical

C. supportive

D. not mentioned

New Words and Phrases

Text A:

misguided [ˌmɪsˈgaɪdɪd] *adj.* 被误导的；搞错的；误入歧途的 *v.* 使入歧途（misguide 的过去分词）

e.g.1. The author raises some questions misguided about the definition and classification of the cosmetics.

作者提出了在化妆品定义与分类方面存在的很多误导问题。

e.g. 2. His plan of attack was misguided.

他的进攻计划被误导了。

eliminate [ɪˈlɪmɪneɪt] *v.* 排除；清除；淘汰；消灭

e.g. 1. This diet claims to eliminate toxins from the body.

这种饮食据称具有排除体内毒素的作用。

e.g. 2. We must eliminate these obstacles.

我们要消除障碍。

illogic [ɪˈlɒdʒɪk] *n.* 不合逻辑，缺乏逻辑的思想

e.g. They threw their King Kong together with an unthinking haste that accounts for its zany illogic.

他们不假思索地匆匆把金刚凑在一起，这也解释了它滑稽可笑的原因。

relevant [ˈreləvənt] *adj.* 相关的；合适的；有意义的

a relevant suggestion/question/point 相关的提议 / 问题 / 观点

e.g. 1. These comments are not directly relevant to this enquiry.
这些意见与这项调查没有直接联系。
e.g. 2. Do you have the relevant experience?
你有相关的经历吗？
scenario [sə'nɑːriəʊ] *n.* 设想；可能发生的情况；剧情梗概
e.g. 1. Let me suggest a possible scenario.
我来设想一种可能出现的情况。
e.g. 2. In this scenario, a compiler uses reflection emit to compile regular expressions in source code.
在此方案中，编译器使用反射发射来编译源代码中的正则表达式。
premise ['premɪs] *n.* 前提，假设；上述各项
a false premise 错误的前提
e.g. The programme started from the premise that men and women are on equal terms in this society.
这个项目是以社会男女平等为前提的。
dictate [dɪk'teɪt] *vt.* 口述；命令，指示；使听写；控制，支配 *n.* 命令；指示；指导原则
e.g. 1. She refused to be dictated to by anyone.
她不愿受任何人摆布。
e.g. 2. In modern western societies, however, the focus on individuality and independence means that people are less concerned about conforming to the dictates of family and culture.
然而，在现代西方社会，对个性和独立的关注意味着人们不太关心遵守家庭和文化的规定。
boost [buːst] *v.* 使增长，推动；增强，提高 *n.* 帮助，激励；增长，提高；向上一推
to boost exports/profits 增加出口；提高利润
to boost sb's confidence/morale 增强某人的信心 / 士气
e.g. Winning the competition was a wonderful boost for her morale.
赢得了那场比赛使她士气大振。
interact [ˌɪntər'ækt] *v.* 交流，互动；相互作用

e.g. 1. Atoms within the fluid interact with the minerals that form the grains.
液体中的原子与形成颗粒的矿物质相互作用。
e.g. 2. There are various ways in which individual economic units can interact with one another.
各个经济单位有许多不同的方式相互作用。
foe [fəʊ] *n.* 敌人，仇敌；危害物；反对者
e.g. 1. A friend is a friend; a foe is a foe; one must be clearly distinguished from the other.
敌是敌，友是友，必须分清界限。
e.g. 2. Hatred with friend is succour to foe.
亲者痛，仇者快。
curtail [kɜːˈteɪl] *v.* 限制；缩短；减缩
e.g. 1. Spending on books has been severely curtailed.
购书开支已被大大削减。
e.g. 2. The lecture was curtailed by the fire alarm going off.
那次讲座因突然鸣响的火警中断了。
simultaneous [sɪm(ə)lˈteɪniəs] *adj.* 同时发生的；同时存在的；同时的；联立的
simultaneous translation/interpreting 同声传译
e.g. There were several simultaneous attacks by the rebels.
反叛者同时发动了几次攻击。
disdain [dɪsˈdeɪn] *n.* 鄙视；轻蔑 *vt.* 鄙视；不屑于做；不愿意做
e.g. 1. Franklin told Sara that he had himself disdained to take the job.
富兰克林告诉萨拉他不屑于去做那份工作。
e.g. 2. Janet looked at him with disdain.
珍妮特轻蔑地看着他。
amplify [ˈæmplɪfaɪ] *v.* 放大；增强；充实
amplify a guitar/an electric current/a signal 放大吉他声音 / 电流 / 信号
e.g. You may need to amplify this point.
你可能需要对这一点进一步予以说明。
more often than not 往往；在大多数情况下
e.g. 1. More often than not she misses the bus.

她经常赶不上这班公共汽车。

e.g. 2. More often than not the patient recovers.

病人多半能恢复健康。

with certainty 确信；肯定

e.g. 1. I do not know with certainty if Mark will be at home tomorrow.

我并不确定马克明天是否在家。

e.g. 2. I can say with certainty (that) she is qualified for the position.

我可以肯定地说，她适合这个职位。

for no (apparent) reason 无缘无故；没有（明确的）原因

e.g. 1. For no reason at all the two men started to laugh.

两个人莫名其妙地开始大笑。

e.g. 2. His boss often swore at him, sometimes for no reason at all.

老板经常骂他，有时毫无理由。

stay away from sb./sth. 离开，不接近（某人）；与……保持距离

e.g. 1. To lose weight, you should stay away from rich food.

你要减肥，就别吃油腻食品。

e.g. 2. In any case he was going to stay away from the General.

反正他要尽量离将军远一些。

stick to sth. 信守；遵守；坚守

e.g. 1. Remember, stick to the issues and don't take it personally.

记住，就事论事，不要把问题个人化。

e.g. 2. I'm not a fashion victim; I stick to what suits me.

我不是一味赶时髦的人，我只穿适合自己的服装。

get on with sth. 开展，进行（某事）

e.g. 1. I was able to get on with my work without interruption.

我可以不受打扰继续我的工作了。

e.g. 2. What are your neighbours like? Do you get on with them?

你的邻居怎么样？跟他们相处得好吗？

Text B

Warming-up Activity:

Pre-reading Questions:

1. Do you know about the scientist Tu Youyou? Do you know other female scientists? Please have a group discussion on female scientists.
2. Why does the author want to talk about the phrase "Woman scientist"?

Why Does the Phrase "Woman Scientist" Even Existed

It's ungrammatical—plus, it suggests we're an exotic species. But it can also remind people that STEM isn't just for men.

By Rachel Lance

Recently, NASA has been working to erase all hints of gender bias lingering from previous generations. The Agency even converted the phrase "manned mission" to "crewed mission", and stood by the change for the recent SpaceX launch, despite the fact that both members of the crew possessed their very own Y chromosomes. Casual English speech is riddled with gender-specific terms like "manned" that we now use without deliberate bias or sexism but that sometimes carry inadvertent shadows of past decades' antiquated stereotypes. Many of them leave me scratching my head to figure out why we need to mention gender at all.

Unsurprisingly, the swap to the neutral "crewed" caused some petulant foot-stamping in internet comments sections, because traditional male-specific phrases seem to stick most insistently in fields that are still perceived as male-dominated. Nobody ever protests that an elementary school should be described as "manned" instead of "staffed", but dare to suggest a "men at work" sign could just as easily read "workers present" and you might spark a kerfuffle. However, the growing number of women who fill these allegedly macho jobs are starting to speak up, and to push for gender neutrality in language. It's possible the phrase "giant leap for mankind" would now reference "humanity" instead, because of socially aware modernday NASA professionals.

But in many cases women are still subtly identified as outsiders. For fields stereotyped as male, like science, medicine or firefighting, we often create special two-noun phrases to describe the women storming the ivory towers of manliness: woman scientist, woman doctor, woman firefighter. To begin with, these peculiar two-noun phrases are grammatically incorrect. The right way to modify the nouns scientist, doctor and firefighter is with an adjective, for example the word "female," as in female doctor. Unless, of course, we mean that a "woman scientist" is somehow an entirely different creature than a normal scientist. Some protest that the word "female" sounds clinical, but notably the grammatical mistake never occurs in reverse, even for men in traditionally female roles; we always manage correctly to apply the adjective "male", as in "a male nurse" rather than "a man nurse".

A search of the online database Newspapers.com shows that prior to the turn of the century the phrase "woman scientist" was used a sparse 40 times in total, peppered throughout multiple decades. The highest concentration was a light smattering of articles about one Jennie A. Estes, who showed up and existed at a scientific meeting in 1897.

But then, enter Marie Curie. The trailblazing genius and her husband were awarded the Nobel Prize, the first time the award had ever been given to a woman, and by 1906, when she became a professor with a lab, she could no longer be ignored. Immediately, the term "woman scientist" exploded into the media, going from a bare trickle of women discussed as curiosities to a sudden flood of articles, with nearly a thousand uses over the next decade.

Some of the articles were supportive, describing Curie as an exotic but admirable specimen. The majority of journalists, however, wondered if woman scientists could possibly have "any manners" at all; attributed their work to male partners; or quipped that women in science were "as rare as the dodo", which as you'll recall is a bird famous for its extinction. Many articles had cautionary titles seemingly designed to scare off women inspired by Curie, such as "Intellectual Powers Could Not Compensate for Loss of Suitor". To me, the subtext seems clear:"woman scientists"are less than, as both women and as scientists.

After this, such phrases began to bloom in other conventionally masculine fields, with newspaper stories about the fashion choices of "woman pilots" who dared to wear pants, and "woman firefighters" who somehow would be physically capable of operating engines. The increasing genesis of two-noun woman phrases correlated with a growing presence in the papers of another gender-shaking, world-altering word: suffrage. After women were granted the right to vote in 1920, the woman phrases dipped in popularity before a resurgence with post-World War II feminism.

The filed of aviation is unique in that the women themselves have embraced their two-noun term—to a degree. Pilot and historian Katherine Sharp Landdeck, author of *The Women with Silver Wings*, a book about the Women Airforce Service Pilots (WASPs) of WWII, says she belongs to the group Women Military Aviators and used to read *Woman Pilot* magazine. She doesn't think the trend traces directly to the legendary WASPs, though, who were named in part because co-founder Jackie Cochran wanted to be clear the women were not trying to replace the "normal" pilots. Rather, Landdeck thinks the term "woman pilot" originated outside the influence of the early female aviators themselves, and is reflective of the more general linguistic trend of outside observers applying two-noun phrases to trailblazing women. However, she does note that many women in aviation are willing to use the phrase as part of an ongoing effort to encourage more equality in a world where a mere 7 percent of participants are female.

And Landdeck has a point. As she says, "if you can't see it, you can't be it." She's never heard a woman introduce herself as "a woman pilot", just as I've never heard a scientific colleague introduce herself as "a woman scientist", but our very existence makes us "stand out nonetheless". I've been called two-noun woman phrases too, by people pointing out my rarity, as my doctorate in blast trauma often renders me a gender oddity in my profession as well as a social oddity at cocktail parties. Recently the phrase "woman scientist" even eked itself without my permission into library catalog descriptions of my book *In the Waves*, which is about blast science and the civil War submarine H. L. Hunley, and which contains not one discussion of gender.

In fields where women remain the few, the odd ducks, the anomalous outliers who constantly have to justify to others our passions for our "manly" fields, I will admit there is sometimes value in pointing out our existence to younger generations when it is relevant to do so. Perhaps it will help one or two young women feel more normal about their inherent love of math or airplanes. But maybe, as society slowly edges toward equality, we can at least start to be more equal in our language too, like NASA and dispose of the grammatically incorrect two-noun woman phrases. Grammarian Mignon Fogarty recommends a simple test: ask yourself if you would phrase the sentence the same way if your subject were a man. If you would use "male" instead of "man", then use "female" instead of "woman". If you would omit his gender altogether, then consider whether mentioning her gender is necessary. It certainly wouldn't be a giant leap for mankind, but it might be a tiny nudge for humanity.

Rachel Lance, Ph.D., is a woman scientist and the author of *In the Waves: My Quest to Solve the Mystery of a Civil War Submarine*. She would like to thank her man friend Kevin for pointing two-noun woman phrases out to her, as she, too, used to use them accidentally.

Reading Exercises:

Check whether each statement is true (T) or false (F).

1. "Woman scientist" is both grammatically correct and gender neutral.
2. We use gender-specific terms in casual English speech unconsciously, but affected by past's stereotypes.
3. Traditional male-specific phrases seem to stick most insistently in fields that are still perceived as male-dominated, so the sign "men at work" reveals gender neutrality.
4. The "ivory towers" in Para.3 means fields only for men.

5. Jennie A. Estes is a figure mostly been called “woman scientists” after 1900.

New Words and Phrases

Text B:

phrase [freɪz] *n.* 惯用法；词组 *v.* 用语言表达

a memorable phrase 易记的警句

e.g. 1. She was, in her own favourite phrase, “a woman without a past”.

用她自己最喜欢的字眼说，她是“一个没有过去的女人”。

e.g. 2. The speech was carefully phrased.

该演讲措辞严谨。

linger [ˈlɪŋɡə(r)] *vi.* 逗留，徘徊；缓慢消失

e.g. 1. The civil war lingered on well into the 1930s.

这次内战到 20 世纪 30 年代还拖了好几年。

e.g. 2. Don’t linger away your holidays. Try to find something useful to do.

不要虚度假日，尽量找些有意义的事做。

convert [kənˈvɜːt] *v.*（使）转变；改造；换算；（使）改变信仰；使……迷上 *n.* 皈依者；改变宗教信仰者；刚迷上……的人

e.g. 1. The hotel is going to be converted into a nursing home.

那家旅馆将被改建成私人疗养院。

e.g. 2. What rate will I get if I convert my dollars into euros?

如果我把美元兑换成欧元，汇率是多少？

manned [mænd] *adj.*（指机器）有人控制的；载人

manned space flight 载人航天

e.g. In thirty years from now the United States should have a manned spacecraft on Mars.

未来 30 年内，美国有可能会把载人航天器送上火星。

sexism [ˈseksɪzəm] *n.* 性别歧视；男性至上主义

e.g. They work hard for a multiracial and multicultural society and sexism.

她们为拥有一个男女平等、各民族平等共处、多元文化共存共荣的未来社会努力奋斗。

perceive [pəˈsiːv] *v.* 意识到；察觉，发觉；理解

e.g. 1. I perceived a change in his behaviour.

我注意到他举止有些变化。

e.g. 2. "Precisely what other problems do you perceive?" she asked.

"你究竟还发现了什么问题？" 她问道。

allegedly [əˈledʒɪdlɪ] *adv.* 据说，据称

e.g. 1. He is allegedly a police agent.

据传他是警方的密探。

e.g. 2. What did you do with the money Mr. Lucas allegedly paid you?

你把卢卡斯承诺给你的钱都用在哪里了？

manliness [ˈmænlɪnəs] *n.* 刚毅

e.g. 1. He has no doubts about his manliness.

他毫不怀疑自己的男人气概。

e.g. 2. She was really fond of his strength, his wholesome looks, his manliness.

她真喜欢他的坚强，他那健康的容貌，他的男子气概。

resurgence [rɪˈsɜːdʒəns] *n.* 复苏，复活；中断之后的继续；再起；回潮

a period of economic resurgence 经济复苏时期

e.g. A resurgence of his grief swept over Nim.

悲痛又涌上了尼姆的心头。

ongoing [ˈɒngəʊɪŋ] *adj.* 不间断的，进行的；前进的

an ongoing debate/discussion/process 持续的辩论 / 讨论 / 过程

e.g. 1. The police investigation is ongoing.

警方的调查在持续进行中。

e.g. 2. There is an ongoing debate on the issue.

对此问题的争论一直没有间断过。

stand by sth. 遵守诺言（或协议等）

e.g. 1. He continues to insist that all he wrote in the book is nothing but the truth, and that he will stand by his word.

他仍坚持说，他在书里写的全都是事实，他会信守自己说过的话。

e.g. 2. Stand by for further orders!

准备好待命！

be riddled with sth. 充满；充斥

a speech riddled with lies 充满谎言的演讲

speak up (for sb./ sth.) 明确表态；（尤指为……）说好话，辩护

e.g. Uncle Herbert never argued, never spoke up for himself.

赫伯特叔叔从不与人争吵，也从不为自己辩护。

in reverse 反向；相反

e.g. 1. Amis tells the story in reverse, from the moment the man dies.

埃米斯以倒叙的方式讲述了这个故事，从这个男人死去的时候开始讲起。

e.g. 2. Please read the names on this list in reverse order.

请看看这张单子上的名字，先从末尾看起。

scare off 把（人）吓倒，使……害怕

e.g. Keep quiet, or you'll scare off away the bird.

安静，要不然你就把那只鸟给吓跑了。

stand out 突出；坚持；超群；向前跨步

e.g. 1. Grammatical errors are always obvious to me, spelling mistakes stand out.

语法错误对我来说总是非常明显，而拼写错误也很显眼。

e.g. 2. He played the violin, and he stood out from all the other musicians...

他演奏了小提琴，把其他所有乐师都比了下去。

dispose of 去掉；清除；销毁

e.g. 1. We will have to dispose of the mice in the attic.

我们必须消灭阁楼里的老鼠。

e.g. 2. These goods are difficult to dispose of.

这些货不好脱手。

Writing

范文赏析

Dear President,

I am Chen Ming, one of the sophomore students in our university. I saw that our Student Union post a notice collecting advice about enriching extracurricular activities, so I am writing this letter to make some suggestions.

First, could you organize more sports activities? Now, there is only one annual school-wide sports meet, and I believe both the variety and the frequency of such events can be increased to better promote the students' physical and mental development. Second, it might be a good idea for our students to engage in more social activities which can broaden our horizons and improve our sense of responsibilities. The Student Union can recruit volunteers to aid rural Project Hope primary schools, go to nursing homes to visit elderly people, and raise funds to help disadvantaged groups. Besides, I suggest that more distinguished experts and scholars in distinct fields be invited to deliver speeches to our students. Last year, the Student Union organized a couple of forums and lectures, which received wide acclaim from both teachers and students in our school.

Thank you for your time, and I believe our Student Union will play a bigger role in enriching our students' mind by organizing colorful and diversified extracurricular activities.

Yours sincerely,

Chen Ming

Vocabulary Exercises

A. *Fill in the blanks with the words in the box. Read the sentences carefully before making your choices. You may not use any of the words in the bank more than once. Change the form where necessary.*

misguided premise dictate interact disdain amplify linger convert manned allegedly

1. Teachers need to ________ with each child.
2. The faint smell of her perfume ________ in the room.
3. He is working on sending a ________ spaceship to Mars.
4. Health is the ________ of success.
5. What right has one country to ________ the environmental standards of another?
6. You are deceiving yourself; you are completely ________.
7. He ________ to turn to his son for advice.
8. You may need to ________ this point.

9. I didn't use to like opera but my husband has ________ me.

10. Meg Ryan is under arrest for ________ embezzling funds from the company.

B. *Fill in the blanks with the phrases in the box. Read the sentences carefully before making your choices. You may not use any of the phrases in the bank more than once. Change the form where necessary.*

more often than not	with certainty	for no reason	stay away from	get on with
stand by	be riddled with	speak up	scare off	stand out

1. I was able to ___________ my work without interruption.
2. Mr. Who? Could you ___________, please?
3. He continues to insist that all he wrote in the book is nothing but the truth, and that he will ___________ his word.
4. Ben is a fairly good runner, he wins ___________.
5. ___________ at all the two men started to laugh.
6. He played the violin, and he ___________ from all the other musicians.
7. The doctor told him to ___________ fat food.
8. The report ___________ errors.
9. If you make a noise, you'll ___________ the animals.
10. I do not know ___________ if Mark will be at home tomorrow.

Extended Exercises

Cloze

There is a passage with 10 blanks. You are required to select one word for each blank from a list of choices in a word bank following the passage. Read the passage through carefully before making your choices. Each choice in the bank is identified by a letter.

A) accessible	B) accounted	C) adaptation	D) appropriately
E) considerable	F) effective	G) ladder	H) misread
I) nomination	J) overlooked	K) promoting	L) senior
M) submission	N) suggesting	O) thankfully	

"Science and everyday life cannot and should not be separated." Those were the words uttered by pioneering British scientist Rosalind Franklin, who firmly believed that the pursuit of science should be __1__ to all.

As a woman working in the first half of the 20th century, Franklin's contributions to some of the greatest scientific discoveries of our time including the structure of DNA — were sadly __2__ in her lifetime.

More than 60 years after Franklin's death, we are __3__ living in a different world, where women play an important part in every echelon (阶层) of our society—not least in science, innovation, higher education and research. UK universities are world leaders when it comes to advancing and __4__ gender equality.

In the past decade, we have seen a __5__ increase in England in the number of women accepted on to full-time undergraduate degrees in science, technology, engineering and maths (Stem subjects). And in the last academic year, women __6__ for more than half of all Stem postgraduates at UK universities.

Data shows us the __7__ to success gets harder for women to climb the further up they go. Although women make up the majority of undergraduates in our universities, just under half of academic staff are female. At __8__ levels, only a quarter of professors are women, and black women make up less than 2% of all female academic staff.

There are also stark differences in pay across grades. The gender pay gap based on median salaries across the sector in 2016 - 2017 was 13. 7%, __9__ there is still some way to go to ensure women are rising through the ranks to higher grade positions and being paid __10__.

Paragraph Matching

You are going to read a passage with ten statements attached to it. Each statement contains information given in one of the paragraphs. Identify the paragraph from which the information is derived. You may choose a paragraph more than once. Each paragraph is marked with a letter.

How to Eat Well

[A] Why do so many Americans eat tons of processed food, the stuff that is correctly called junk（垃圾）and should really carry warning labels?

[B] It's not because fresh ingredients are hard to come by. Supermarkets offer more variety than ever, and there are over four times as many farmers' markets in the US as there were 20 years ago. Nor is it for lack of available information. There are plenty of recipes（食谱）, how-to videos and cooking classes available to anyone who has a computer, smart phone or television. If anything, the information is overwhelming.

[C] And yet we aren't cooking. If you eat three meals a day and behave like most Americans, you probably get at least a third of your daily calories（卡路里）outside the home. Nearly two-thirds of us grab fast food once a week, and we get almost 25% of our daily calories from snacks. So we're eating out or taking in, and we don't sit down or we do, but we hurry.

[D] Shouldn't preparing and consuming food be a source of comfort, pride, health, well-being, relaxation, sociability? Something that connects us to other humans? Why would we want to outsource（外包）this basic task, especially when outsourcing it is so harmful?

[E] When I talk about cooking, I'm not talking about creating elaborate dinner parties or three-day science projects. I'm talking about simple, easy, everyday meals. My mission is to encourage green hands and those lacking time or money to feed themselves. That means we need modest, realistic expectations, and we need to teach people to cook food that's good enough to share with family and friends.

[F] Perhaps a return to real cooking needn't be far off. A recent Harris poll revealed that 79% of Americans say they enjoy cooking and 30% "love it"; 14% admit to not enjoying kitchen work and just 7% won't go near the stove at all. But this doesn't necessarily translate to real cooking, and the result of this survey shouldn't surprise anyone: 52% of those 65 or older cook at home five or more times per week; only a third of young people do.

[G] Back in the 1950s most of us grew up in households where mom cooked virtually every night. The intention to put a home-cooked meal on the table was pretty much universal. Most people couldn't afford to do otherwise.

[H] Although frozen dinners were invented in the 40s, their popularity didn't boom until televisions became popular a decade or so later. Since then, packaged, pre-prepared meals have been what's for dinner. The microwave and fast-food chains were the biggest catalysts（催化剂）, but the big food companies—which want to sell anything except the raw ingredients that go into cooking—made the home cook an endangered species .

[I] Still, I find it strange that only a third of young people report preparing meals at home regularly. Isn't this the same crowd that rails against processed junk and champions craft cooking? And isn't this the generation who say they're concerned about their health and the well-being of the planet? If these are truly the values of many young people, then their behavior doesn't match their beliefs.

[J] There have been half-hearted but well-publicized efforts by some food companies to reduce calories in their processed foods, but the standard American Diet is still the Polar opposite of the healthy, mostly plant- based diet that just about every expert says we should be eating. Considering that the government's standards are not nearly ambitious enough, the picture is clear: by not cooking at home, we're not eating the right things, and the consequences are hard to overstate.

[K] To help quantify（量化）the costs of a Poor diet, I recently tried to estimate this impact in terms of a most famous food, the burger（汉堡包）. I concluded that the profit from burgers is more than offset（抵消）by the damage they cause in health problems and environmental harm.

[L] Cooking real food is the best defense—not to mention that any meal you're likely to eat at home contains about 200 fewer calories than one you would eat in a restaurant.

[M] To those Americans for whom money is a concern, my advice is simple: Buy what you can afford, and cook it yourself. The common prescription is to Primarily shop the grocery store, since that's where fresh produce, meat and seafood, and dairy are. And to save money and still eat well you don't need local, organic ingredients; all you need is real food. I'm not saying local food isn't better; it is. But there is plenty of decent food in the grocery stores.

[N] The other sections you should get to know are the frozen foods and the canned goods. Frozen Produce is still produce; canned tomatoes are still tomatoes. Just make sure you're getting real food without tons of added salt or sugar. Ask yourself, would grandma consider this food? Does it look like something that might occur in nature? It's Pretty much common sense: you want to buy food, not unidentifiable food like objects.

[O] You don't have to hit the grocery store daily, nor do you need an abundance of skill. Since fewer than half of Americans say they cook at an intermediate level and only 20% describe their cooking skills as advanced, the crisis is one of confidence. And the only remedy for that is practice. There's nothing mysterious about cooking the evening meal. You just have to do a little thinking ahead and redefine what qualifies as dinner. Like any skill, cooking gets easier as you do it more; every time you cook, you advance your level of skills. Someday you won't even need recipes. My advice is that you not pay attention to the number of steps and ingredients, because they can be deceiving.

[P] Time, I realize, is the biggest obstacle to cooking for most people. You must adjust your priorities to find time to cook. For instance, you can move a TV to the kitchen and watch your favorite shows while you're standing at the sink. No one is asking you to give up activities you like, but if you're watching food shows on TV, try cooking instead.

1. Cooking benefits People in many ways and enables them to connect with one another.
2. Abundant information about cooking is available either online or on TV.

3. Young people do less cooking at home than the elderly these days.
4. Cooking skills can be improved with practice.
5. In the mid-20th century, most families ate dinner at home instead of eating out.
6. Even those short of time or money should be encouraged to cook for themselves and their family.
7. Eating food not cooked by ourselves can cause serious consequences.
8. To eat well and still save money, people should buy fresh food and cook it themselves.
9. We get a fairly large portion of calories from fast food and snacks.
10. The popularity of TV led to the popularity of frozen food.

Cultural Translation

Directions: *For this part, you are allowed 30 minutes to translate a passage from Chinese into English.*

故宫（The Forbidden City）雄伟、壮丽，是中国古建筑艺术的巅峰之作，其规模和独具特色的风格享誉世界。故宫内保存着大量珍贵、稀有的古物，它们对研究明、清两代历史和历代艺术具有十分重要的意义。1925 年故宫改名为故宫博物院，并成为世界上最大的博物馆之一。新中国成立后，人民政府投入了大量资金对故宫进行保护和维修。它现在是北京最受欢迎的旅游景点之一。

练习答案

Reading Exercises

Text A: 1 ～ 5 BBCBC

Text B: 1 ～ 5 FTFTF

Vocabulary Exercises

A:

1. interact
2. lingered
3. manned
4. premise
5. dictate
6. misguided
7. disdained
8. amplify
9. converted
10. allegedly

B:

1. get on with
2. speak up
3. stand by
4. more often than not
5. For no reason
6. stood out
7. stay away from
8. was riddled with
9. scare off
10. with certainty

Extended Exercises

Cloze:

1 ～ 10: AJOKE BGLND

Paragraph Matching:

1 ～ 10: DBFOG EJMCH

Cultural Translation:

The Forbidden City is majestic and magnificent. It is the pinnacle of Chinese ancient architecture art and enjoys worldwide fame for its scale and unique style. The Forbidden City has a large number of precious and rare ancient relics, which are of great significance to the study of the history and art of the Ming and Qing dynasties. In 1925, it was renamed the Palace Museum and became one of the largest museums in the world. After the founding of People's Republic of China, the people's government invested a lot of money to protect and repair the Forbidden City. It is now one of the most popular tourist attractions in Beijing.

Unit 8 English Literature

Part 1 A Brief Introduction to British Literature

British literature is the quintessence of British culture made by its people throughout years of the country's development. Reading British literary works can enable readers to gain deeper insights into its culture, which help to blend Chinese and western culture, and implement Quality Education.

1 English Literature In the Old and Middle Ages

1. 1 The Old English Period (449—1066)

The most important work of Old English literature is *Beowulf*—the national epic of the English people.

1. 2 The Middle English Period (1066—1485)

In 1066, the Normans conquered England. During the period that followed the Conquest, French literature expanded. Romances were the most prevalent kind of literature in the period, among which *Sir Gawain* and *the Green Knight* were considered the most popular.

The greatest poet of the Middle English is Geoffrey Chaucer, the father of English poetry. Chaucer was the first one to introduce the Heroic Couplet into English literature, that is, lines of iambic pentameter which rhyme in pairs: aa, bb, cc and so on.

2 The Renaissance (1485—1660)

The Renaissance began in the 14th century in Italy. Renaissance reached England late. The Beginning of the English Renaissance is often taken to be 1485, and the Elizabethan era in the second half of the 16th century is usually regarded as the height of the English Renaissance.

Thomas More is one of the most remarkable humanists in the English Renaissance. His Latin prose narrative *Utopia* satirizes the irrationality of inherited assumptions about private property and money. More's book describes a distant nation organized on purely reasonable principles and named Utopia, which means nowhere in Greek.

Edmund Spencer's masterpiece *Faerie Queen* is one of the most famous works of the English Renaissance. The Spenserian sonnet is a lyric poem consisting of three quatrains and a concluding couplet: abab bcbc cdcd ee.

Christopher Marlowe was the greatest pioneer of English drama. His representatives are *Tamburlaine*, *Doctor Faustus*, *The Jew of Malta*.

William Shakespeare was the greatest English poet and dramatist. He has left us a great wealth of 2 long poems, 154 sonnets as well as 39 plays. He produced his best history plays: *Henry IV*, *Comedies*: *A Midsummer Night's Dream*, *The Merchant of Venice*, *Greatest tragedies: Hamlet*, *Othello*, *King Lear*, *Macbeth*, and *Play of dramatic romances: the Tempest*.

Ben Jonson, the greatest writer of comedy after Shakespeare. His acknowledged masterpieces are *Volpone* and *The Alchemist*.

Francis Bacon's Essays won him a high place in the history of English literature.

John Donne, the father of Metaphysical poetry, together with Andrew Marvell was famous for Metaphysical poetry.

John Milton wrote *Paradise Lost*, *Paradise Regained and Samson Agonistes*. *Paradise Lost* mainly tells the machinations of Satan, the Devil, leading to the fall of Adam and Eve from the state of innocence; and he performed the task in such a way as to "justify the ways of God to man" and to express the central Christian truths of freedom, sin, and redemption.

John Bunyan's masterpiece is his prose work *The Pilgrim's Progress*.

John Dryden was the dominant literary figure and influence of his age. He established the heroic couplet as the standard meter of English poetry, by writing successful satires, fables, epigrams, compliments, prologues, and plays in it.

3 The Restoration and the Eighteenth Century (1660—1798)

Richard Steel and Joseph Addison helped published articles with different subjects through *Tatler* and *Spectator*.

Jonathan Swif produced *Gulliver's Travels*. The novel is a known satire.

Samuel Richardson is famous for *Pamela* and *Clarissa*.

Tobias Smollett wrote *The Adventures of Roderick Random*.

Lawrence Stern's *Tristram Shandy* is known as the most typical novel of world literature for the innovative novel-writing skills such as inserting sermons, essays and legal documents, marbled pages and, most famously, an entirely black page within the narrative, into the pages of his novel.

There were many literature trends in the 18th century England, Neo-classism, Realistic novel, and Sentimentalism.

3. 1 Neoclassicism

In late 17th and early 18th century England, the dominant literary theory was Neoclassicism.

In England, neoclassicism was initiated by John Dryden, culminated in Alexander Pope and continued by Samuel Johnson.

Alexander Pope was a representative figure of neoclassic poetry. And he was also noted for his translation of the great epic poem *Iliad*.

Samuel Johnson was remembered for *Lives of the Poets*, *The Preface to Shakespeare* as well as compiling the very first English dictionary, *Dictionary of the English Language.*

3. 2 The Realistic Novel

Daniel Defoe was known as the Father of English novel for *Robison Crusoe*, which tells of a man's shipwreck on a deserted island and his subsequent adventures with the leading character Crusoe and Friday.

3. 3 Sentimentalism

Sentimentalism was one of the important trends in English literature of the middle and later decades of the 18th century.

Oliver Goldsmith wrote *The Deserted Village*.

James Thomson produced *The Seasons*.

Thomas Gray is the author of *Elegy Written in a Country Churchyard*.

William Collins' *Ode to Evening* is also a representative work of sentimentalism.

4 The Age of Romanticism (1798—1832)

4. 1 Poetry

Romanticism is a literary trend, which was greatly influenced by the Industrial Revolution and the French Revolution.William Blake and Robert Burns are usually called the poets of Pre-romanticism.

William Blake's most important poetic works are *Songs of Innocence*, and *Songs of Experience*.

Robert Burns was the national poet of Scotland, and was famous for his poems: *A Red, Red Rose, Auld Lang Syne*.

The Romantic Age began in 1798 when William Wordsworth and Samuel Taylor Coleridge published *Lyrical Ballads* (The statement that poetry is the spontaneous overflow of powerful feelings, was in the preface to *Lyrical Ballads*).

Key figures of the Romantic movement include such poets: Passive Romantic poets represented by the Lakers / Lake Poets-William Wordsworth, Samuel Taylor Coleridge, Robert Southey and Active / Revolutionary Romantic poets represented by those younger poets—George Gordon Byron, Percy Bysshe Shelley and John Keats.

William Wordsworth wrote his principal poems : *The Prelude*, *Lyrical Ballads*, and *The Excursion*.

Samuel Taylor Coleridge's masterpieces are *The Rime of the Ancient Mariner, Kubla Khan and Christabel*.

George Gordon Byron was made famous chiefly by his *Childe Harold's*

Pilgrimage, and *Don Juan*.

Percy Bysshe Shelley's *Prometheus Unbound*, *Ode to the West Wind*, *To a Skylark*, *The Cloud*, *Adonais* (*The Elegy for John Keats*) are regarded as his masterpieces.

John Keats is known to the majority by his poems *On a Grecian Urn*, *To a Nightingale*, *Old to Autumn and The Eve of St. Agnes*.

4. 2 Non-Poetic Literature of the Age

4. 2. 1 Essay

Charles Lamb's important works include *Essays of Elia*, and *Tales from Shakespeare*.

William Hazlitt was remembered for his literary criticism, and his chief critical work is *Characters of Shakespeare's Play*.

4. 2. 2 Novel

Jane Austen wrote six novels all together, among which *Pride and Prejudice*, *Sense and Sensibility and Emma* are considered as her masterpieces.

Sir Walter Scott's *The Lady of the Lake* won him great fame as a poet, and his chiefly famous novels are *The Heart of Midlothian and Ivanhoe*.

5 The Victorian Age (1837—1901)

5. 1 Poetry

Alfred Tennyson was a representative poet of the Victorian Age. His works include *In Memoriam*, *The Idylls of the King*.

Robert Browning, English poet, was noted for his mastery of dramatic monologue. His best works are *The Ring and the Book*, *Dramatic Romances and Lyrics*, *Pippa Passes*.

Matthew Arnold was a poet and an important literary critic in this age. His major works are *Essays in Criticism*, *Stanzas from the Grande Chartreuse*.

5. 2 Novel

Charles Dickens gave readers a realistic and vivid picture of the English society of his age, among his different novels, *Oliver Twist*, *David Copperfield*, *Great Expectations and A Tale of Two Cities* won him great reputation.

William Makepeace Thackeray produced *Vanity Fair* and *The History of Henry Esmond*.

George Eliot is the pen-name of Mary Ann Evans. *The Mill on the Floss*, *Silas Marner and Middlemarch* were considered as her representative works.

Charlotte Bronte, Emily Bronte, and Anne Bronte are the famous Bronte sisters.

Charlotte Bronte's best-known literary production is *Jane Eyre*.

Emily Bronte is chiefly remembered for her novel *Wuthering Heights*.

Anne Bronte's *Agnes Grey* is her masterpiece.

Thomas Hardy's the most outstanding novels are *Tess of the D' Urbervilles* and *Jude the Obscure*.

5. 3 Drama

George Bernard Shaw's drama exposed with enormous satirical skill the sickness and fatuities of individuals and societies in England and the rest of the modern world. The best ones are *Widowers' Houses*, *Mrs. Warren's Profession, Major Barbara*, *Pygmalion*, and *Saint Joan*.

6 The Twentieth Century

6. 1 Poetry

William Butler Yeats is an Irish poet. He received the Nobel Prize for Literature in 1923. His chief poetic works include *The Wanderings of Oisin and other poems*, *The Tower*, and *Sailing to Byzantium*.

Thomas Stearns Eliot, together with Yeats, stands at the foremost place of 20th century poetry. He was awarded the Nobel Prize for Literature in 1948. He produced his important poems *The Love Song of J. Alfred Prufrock*, *The Waste Land*, *Four*

Quartets, and the most important of his plays is *Murder in the Cathedral*. The Waste Land is generally considered as the masterpiece of modernist poetry.

6. 2 Novel

John Galsworthy was awarded the Nobel Prize for literature in 1932. His masterpiece is a trilogy, *The Forsyte Saga*, composed of *The Man of Property*, *In Chancery*, and *To Let*.

Arnold Bennett's masterpiece is *The Old Wives' Tale*.

Herbert George Wells produced scientific fantasies, among which *The Time Machine* is of much reputation.

Henry James' well-known novels are *Daisy Miller*, *Portrait of a Lady*, *The Ambassadors*, and *The Golden Bowl*.

Joseph Conrad has his two of his best-known works, *Lord Jim and Heart of Darkness*.

Edward Morgan Forster published his famous novels during his lifetime: *A Room with a View*, *Howard's End*, *A Passage to India*.

D. H. Lawrence has his major novels: *Sons and Lovers*, *The Rainbow*, *Women in Love*, and *Lady Chatterley's Lover*.

James Joyce is an Irish poet and novelist. His *Ulysses* is generally acknowledged to be his masterpiece and a typical example of stream of consciousness technique. His other novels are *Dubliners*, *A Portrait of the Artist as a Young Man*, and *Finnegans Wake*.

Virginia Woolf was noted for her feminist perspective and she was another important exponent of stream of consciousness writing. *Mrs. Dalloway*, *To the Lighthouse*, and *The Waves*, showed her most skillful use of stream of consciousness technique.

Aldous Huxley wrote *Brave New World*.

George Orwell's most popular book is *Animal Farm*, a political satire in fable form on totalitarian society. His last novel, *Nineteen Eighty-four*, predicted social conditions in a highly centralized, tightly-controlled state of the future.

William Golding was awarded the Nobel Prize in 1983. His novel, *Lord of the*

Flies was a great success.

Katherine Mansfield made the short story an important genre of 20th century fiction, and her stories *In a German Pension*, *Bliss*, *The Garden Party*, and *The Dove's Nest* display a striking tendency toward modernism.

Iris Murdock's major works include *Under The Net*, *The Sandcastle*, and *The Bell*.

Doris Lessing has her most popular novel *Golden Notebook*, a feminist novel about intellectual women in modern society, which helped her win the Nobel Prize for Literature in 2007.

6. 3 Drama

Samuel Beckett's *Waiting for Godot* won him public recognition and Beckett was awarded the Nobel Prize in 1969. *Waiting for Godot* is a masterpiece of "Theatre of Absurd".

John Osborn is the most important playwright among the Angry Young Men, and the leader of the dramatic revival which started in the 1950's. His successful play, *Look Back in Anger* reflects the frustration and disappointment of the British post Second World war generation, and their rejection of the established social values and moral standards.

7 Literary terms

Allegory: a narrative or description having a second meaning beneath the surface one

Ballad: a fairly short narrative poem written in a song-like stanzaic form

Blank verse: unrimed iambic pentameter

Canto: sections or divisions of a long poem

Couplet: a unit of verse consisting of two successive lines, usually rhyming and having the same meter.

Criticism: the description, analysis, interpretation, or evaluation of a literary work of art.

Elegy: in its more modern usage, a poem that laments or solemnly meditates on death, loss, or the passing of things of value

Epic: A long narrative poem, elevated and dignified in theme, tone, and style, celebrating heroic deeds and historically (at times cosmically) important events; usually focuses on the adventures of a hero who has qualities that are superhuman or divine and on whose fate very often depends the destiny of a tribe, a nation, or even the whole of the human race

Fable: a story with a moral lesson, often employing animals who talk and act like human beings

Free verse: a type of poetry that deliberately seeks to free itself from the restrictions imposed by traditionally fixed conventions of meter, rhyme, and stanza

Heroic couplet: a pair of rhymed iambic pentameter lines; a stanza composed of two heroic couplets is called a heroic quatrain

Lyric: a short, songlike poem, by a single speaker or a single subject, expressing a personal thought, mood, or feeling

Myth: broadly, any idea or belief to which a number of people subscribe

Narrative poem: a poem that tells a story

Novel: the name generally applied to any long fictional prose narrative

Ode: a long lyric poem, serious and dignified in subject, tone and style, sometimes with an elaborate stanzaic structure, often written to commemorate or celebrate an event or individual

Satire: a kind of literature that ridicules human folly or vice with the purpose of bringing about reform or of keeping others from falling into similar folly or vice

Short story: a short work of narrative prose fiction. The distinction between the short story and novel is mainly one of length

(Mostly adapted from Concise Companion to Literature)

Part 2 Exercises

1. The novel *Emma* is written by______.

A. Mary Shelley B. Charlotte Bronte

C. Elizabeth C. Gaskell D. Jane Austen

2. Which of the following is NOT a romantic poet?

A. William Wordsworth B. George Elliot

C. George G. Byron D. Percy B. Shelley

3. Which of the following writers is a poet of the 20th century?

A. T. S. Eliot B. D. H. Lawrence

C. Theodore Dreiser D. James Joyce

4. Which of the following novels was written by Emily Bronte?

A. *Oliver Twist* B. *Middlemarch*

C. *Jane Eyre* D. *Wuthering Heights*

5. William Butler Yeats was a(n)______poet and playwright.

A. American B. Canadian

C. Irish D. Australian

6. *The Canterbury Tales*, a collection of stories told by a group of pilgrims on their way to Canterbury, is an important poetic work by______.

A. William Langland B. Geoffrey Chaucer

C. William Shakespeare D. Alfred Tennyson

7. All of the following are well-known female writers in 20th-century Britain except_____.

A. George Eliot B. Iris Jean Murdoch

C. Doris Lessing D. Muriel Spark

8. *Ode to the West Wind* was written by_____.

A. William Blake B. William Wordsworth

C. Samuel Taylor Coleridge D. Percy Bysshe Shelley

9. The novel *Sons and Lovers* was written by_____.

A. Thomas Hardy B. John Galsworthy

C. D.H.Lawrence D. James Joyce

10. Who was best known for the technique of dramatic monologue in his poems?

A. Will Blake B. W. B. Yeats

C. Robert Browning D. William Wordsworth

11. In literature, a story in verse or prose with a double meaning is defined as_____.

A. allegory B. sonnet

C. blank verse D. rhyme

12. Virginia Woolf was an important female_____in the 20th-century England.

A. poet B. biographer

C. playwright D. novelist

13. _____refers to a long narrative poem that records the adventures of a hero in a nation's history.

A. Ballad B. Romance

C. Epic D. Elegy

14. *Beowulf* was_____.

A. an Anglo-Saxon epic B. an old English play

C. one of the earliest English novels D. a romantic poem

15. Woolf shares with James Joyce in that many of their works are characteristic of_____.

A. critical realism B. romanticism

C. sentimentalism D. stream of consciousness

16. James Joyce also wrote_____in addition to *Ulysses*.

A. *A Portrait of the Artist as a Young Man* B. *A Passage to India*

C. *The Portrait of a Lady* D. *A Room with a View*

17. *1984* is a novel of political satire written by_____.

A. George Orwell B. Graham Greene

C. William Golding D. Doris Lessing

18. Which of the following statements is true?

A. The author of *Jane Eyre* also wrote *Wuthering Heights*.

B. The author of *Wuthering Heights* and that of *Jane Eyre* were sisters.

C. Charlotte published *Jane Eyre* after Emily did *Wuthering Heights*.

D. *Wuthering Heights* is a sequel to *Jane Eyre*.

19. _____is not a poet of the Victorian era.

A. Robert Browning B. Alfred Tennyson

C. Oliver Goldsmith D. Matthew Arnold

20. _____is the dominant form in the literature during the Victorian age.

A. Poetry B. Novel

C. Drama D. Prose

21. _____and George Bernard Shaw are the milestones on the resurrection of English Drama in the Victorian age.

A. Oscar Wild B. Ben Johnson

C. William Congreve D. Richard Brinsley Sheridan

22. _____is a metaphysical poet of the 17th century.

A. John Donne B. Thomas Gray

C. John Keats D. Ben Johnson

23. _____is a representative work of modernist poetry .

A. *The Waste Land* B. *Sonnets from the Portuguese*

C. *Stanzas from the Grande Chartreuse* D. *In Memoriam*

24. The statement "Poetry is the spontaneous overflow of powerful feelings" was written by_____.

A. William Wordsworth B. Robert Burns

C. William Blake D. Samuel Taylor Coleridge

25. Robert Burns, the writer of *A Red, Red Rose*, is a(n)_____ poet.

A. Irish B. British

C. Scottish D. French

26. _____compiled the first English dictionary.

A. Samuel Johnson B. Walter Scott

C. James Boswell D. Noah Webster

27. *Lord of the Flies* is written by______ .

A. William Golding B. George Orwell

C. Virginia Woolf D. D. H. Lawrence

28. Mary Ann Evans is the pseudonym of_____who wrote *The Mill on the Floss*.

A. George Eliot B. Charlotte Bronte

C. Emily Bronte D. Jane Austen

29. _____ is not one of the modernist writers.

A. Virginia Woolf B. James Joyce

C. T. S. Eliot D. Thomas Hardy

30. _____is not a novel written by James Joyce.

A. *Finnegans Wake* B. *Dubliners*

C. *A Portrait of the Artist as a Yong Man* D. *Women in Love*

31. _____introduced the Heroic Couplet into English literature.

A. Geoffrey Chucer B. Samuel Johnson

C. John Dryden D. William Shakespeare

32. ____ is the climax of Virginia Woolf's experiments through the novel form of "stream of consciousness"

A. *Jacob's Room* B. *To the Lighthouse*

C. *Orlando* D. *The Waves*

33. *Paradise* Lost is written by_____.

A. John Milton B. John Bunyan

C. Christopher Marlow D. John Dryden

34. _____is one of Shakespeare's great tragedies.

A. *Love for Love* B. *Every Man in His Humor*

C. *Hamlet* D. *Twelfth Night*

35. *Essays*, a collection of short articles on a diverse range of subjects, such as death and marriage, ambition and atheism, is written by_____.

A. John Dryden B. Thomas More

C. Francis Bacon D. John Bunyan

36. "To be or not to be, that is a question" is quoted from Shakespeare's famous play_____.

A. *King Lear* B. *Hamlet*

C. *Romeo and Juliet* D. *A Midsummer Night's Dream*

37. The English Renaissance exerts great influence on the following realms EXCEPT_____.

A. politics B. literature

C. philosophy D.education

38. *The Canterbury Tales* is a monumental work of_____.

A. novel B. prose

C. poetry D. drama

39. Thomas More, the great humanist in the Renaissance, was famous for_____.

A. *New Atlantis* B. *Faerie Queen*

C. *Utopia* D. *Samson Agonistes*

40. _____ is an important poet in the 17th century.

A. Geoffrey Chaucer B. Edmund Spenser

C. John Milton D. Francis Bacon

41. *King Lear* is one of Shakespeare's_____.

A. comedies B. histories

C. dramatic romances D. tragedies

42. *Robinson Crusoe* is written by_____.

A. Henry Fielding B. Samuel Richardson

C. Lawrence Sterne D. Daniel Defoe

43. _____is a poet of the 18th century.

A. Alexander Pope B. John Milton

C. Edmund Spenser D. John Donne

44. _____is a representative figure of neo-classism.

A. Alexander Pope B. John Bunyan

C. James Boswell D. Lawrence Sterne

45. Who wrote *The Life and Opinions of Tristram Shandy*?

A. Daniel Defoe B. Jonathan Swift

C. Lawrence Sterne D. Samuel Richardson

46. The rise of British novel was in the_____.

A. 16th century B. 17th century

C. 18th century D. 15th century

47. Sentimentalism is mostly seen in_____.

A. poetry B. novels

C. drama D. romance

48. Which of the following is not written by Yeats?
    A. *Four Quartets*
    B. *A Vision*
    C. *The Winding Stair*
    D. *The Tower*
49. *Songs of Innocence and Songs of Experience* are written by_____.
    A. William Wordsworth
    B. George Gordon Byron
    C. William Blake
    D. Samuel Taylor Coleridge
50. *Auld Lang Syne* is written by______.
    A. William Blake
    B. George Gordon Byron
    C. Robert Burns
    D. John Keats
51. _____is NOT a Revolutionary Romantic poet.
    A. George Gordon Byron
    B. Percy Bysshe Shelley
    C. John Keats
    D. Walter Scott
52. _____is NOT written by Percy Bysshe Shelley.
    A. *Prometheus Unbound*
    B. *Ode to the West Wind*
    C. *Adonais*
    D. *Kubla Khan*
53. _____is a work by the lake poets.
    A. *Don Juan*
    B. *The Rime of the Ancient Mariner*
    C. *Ode on a Grecian Urn*
    D. *To a Skylark*
54. William Hazlitt was famous for his literary criticism on_____.
    A. Shakespeare
    B. John Milton
    C. William Wordsworth
    D. Thomas More
55. ______is NOT written by Charles Lamb.
    A. *Tales from Shakespeare*
    B. *Specimens of English Dramatic Poets*
    C. *Essays of Elia*
    D. *The Preface to Shakespeare*
56. _____is a work by George Gordon Byron.
    A. *Don Juan*
    B. *Prometheus Unbound*
    C. *Lyrical Ballads*
    D. *Ode to a Nightingale*
57. _____is NOT written by William Wordsworth.
    A. *The Prelude*
    B. *Lyrical Ballads*
    C. *To a Skylark*
    D. *The Excursion*

58. *Elegy Written in a Country Churchyard* is a poem written by_____.

A. Oliver Goldsmith B. James Thomson

C. Thomas Gray D. Alexander Pope

59. Which of the following is Not written by D. H. Lawrence?

A. *The Waste Land* B. *The Rainbow*

C. *Lady Chatterley's Lover* D. *Women in Love*

60. _____was a leader of the modernist movement in English poetry and a great innovator of verse technique.

A. Virginia Woolf B. T. S. Eliot

C. D. H. Lawrence D. G. B. Shaw

61. _____is an 18th century novelist.

A. Henry Fielding B. Jane Austen

C. Charles Dickens D. George Eliot

62. _____is NOT a poet of the Victorian era.

A. Robert Browning B. Alfred Tennyson

C. Oliver Goldsmith D. Matthew Arnold

63. _____is NOT a female novelist in the Victorian era.

A. Oliver Twist B. George Eliot

C. Elizabeth Barrett D. Jane Austen

64. _____is NOT written by Charles Dickens.

A. *Oliver Twist* B. *David Copperfield*

C. *Great Expectations* D. *The Mill on the Floss*

65. *Vanity Fair* is written by_____.

A. Charles Dickens B. William Makepeace Thackeray

C. Thomas Hardy D. John Galsworthy

66. Joseph Conrad is the author of_____.

A. *Heart of Darkness* B. *Jude the Obscure*

C. *Agnes Grey* D. *Ivanhoe*

67. Besides *Howards End*, E. M. Forster wrote another famous novel_____.

A. *A Passage to India* B. *The Forsyte Saga*

C. *The History of Henry Esmond* D. *Silas Marner*

68. *Tess of the D' Urbervilles* is considered the best novel of_____.

A. Thomas Hardy B. George Eliot

C. Charles Dickens D. Walter Scott

69. _____is NOT written by a female novelist.

A. *Pride and Prejudice* B. *Ivanhoe*

C. *Jane Eyre* D. *The Mill on the Floss*

70. *Saint Joan* is a play written by_____.

A. John Dryden B. William Gongreve

C. George Bernard Shaw D. Ben Johnson

71. Herbert George Wells is the author of_____, one of the first science fictions.

A. *The Time Machine* B. *Frankenstein*

C. *2000 Leagues under the Sea* D. *Around the World in 80 Days*

72. _____is NOT a novel written by the Bronte sisters.

A. *Wuthering Heights* B. *Emma*

C. *Jane Eyre* D. *Agnes Grey*

73. _____is NOT one of the modernist writers.

A. Virginia Woolf B. James Joyce

C. T. S. Eliot D. Thomas Hardy

74. _____is the masterpiece of James Joyce.

A. *Ulysses* B. *The Plumed Serpent*

C. *Mrs. Dalloway* D. *Lord of the Flies*

75. _____applied a variety of devices of stream-of-consciousness in his literary.

A. D. H. Lawrence B. James Joyce

C. Thomas Hardy D. Joseph Conrad

76. _____is NOT a novel written by James Joyce.

A. *Finnegans Wake* B. *Dubliners*

C. *A Portrait of the Artist as a Young Man* D. *Women in Love*

77. _____is NOT a novel written by Virginia Woolf.

A. *Mrs. Dalloway* B. *Emma*

C. *To the Lighthouse* D. *The Wave*

78. The Waste Land, written by_____, is the greatest modernist poem.

A. T. S. Eliot B.William Butler Yeats

C. Alfred Tennyson D. Matthew Arnold

79. William Butler Yeats is famous for his masterpiece______.

A. *Sailing to Byzantium* B. *The Idylls of the King*

C. *Lyrical Ballads* D. *Prometheus Unbound*

80. _____is NOT a novelist who is famous for applying stream-of-consciousness in the writing.

A. James Joyce B. Virginia Woolf

C. Henry James D. D. H. Lawrence

81. *Animal Farm* is the masterpiece of______.

A. George Orwell B. Virginia Woolf

C. Thomas Hardy D. E. M. Forster

82. _____won the Nobel Prize in 2007 for her novel *The Golden Notebook.*

A. William Butler Yeats B. Jane Austen

C. Doris Lessing D. Iris Jean Murdoch

83. *The Man of Property* is taken from Galsworthy's trilogy, ______.

A. *The End of the Chapter* B. *The Forsyte Saga*

C. *A Modern Comedy* D. *The Island Pharisees*

84. ______is the author of *A Bend in the River*.

A. Doris Lessing B. George Orwell

C. William Golding D. V. S. Naipaul

85. _____, written by John Fowles, is a masterpiece of experimentalism in British literature.

A. *The French Lieutenant's Woman* B. *Nineteen Eighty Four*

C. *A House for Mr. Biswas* D. *The Winding Stair*

86. _____was the first important English woman novelist.

A. Charlotte Bronte B. Jane Austen

C. Virginia Woolf D. George Eliot

87. _____is D. H. Lawrence's semi-autobiographical novel.

A. *Sons and Lovers* B. *Women in Love*

C. *The Plumed Serpent* D. *Lady Chatterley's Lover*

88. Which of the following writers has NOT won the Nobel Prize?

A. William Butler Yeats B. Doris Lessing

C. William Golding D. George Orwell

89. _____is a representative work of modernist poetry.

A. *The Waste Land* B. *Sailing to Byzantium*

C. *Stanzas from the Grande Chartreuse* D. *In Memoriam*

90. ______, the "father of English poetry" and one of the greatest narrative poets of England, was born in London in about 1340.

A. Geoffrey Chaucer B. Sir Gawain

C. Francis Bacon D. John Dryden

91. Chaucer died on October 25th, 1400, and was buried in ____.

A. Flanders B. France

C. Italy D. Westminster Abbey

92. *Utopia* was written in the form of _____.

A. prose B. drama

C. essay D. dialogue

93. Among many poetic forms, Shakespeare was especially at home (good at) with the _______.

A. dramatic blank verse B. song

C. sonnet D. couplet

94. _____has been called the summit of the English Renaissance.

A. Christopher Marlow B. Francis Bacon

C. W. Shakespeare D. Ben Johnson

95. ____was the forerunner of the English classical school of literature in the 18th century.

A. John Dryden B. Richard Steele

C. Joseph Addison D. Alexander Pope

96. Which is the most popular newspaper published by Steele?

A. *The Tatler* B. *The Spectator*

C. *The Theatre* D. *The English*

97. The masterpiece of Alexander Pope is ____.

A. *Essay on Criticism*
B. *The Rape of the Lock*
C. *Essay on Man*
D. *The Dunciad*

98. The main literary stream of the 19th century was ____ . What the writers described in their works were mainly social realities.

A. romanticism
B. classicism
C. realism
D. sentimentalism

99. The 18th century was the golden age of the English ___. The novel of this period spoke the truth about life with an uncompromising (unbending) courage.

A. drama
B. poetry
C. essay
D. novel

100. In a series of pamphlets Jonathan Swift denounced the cruel and unjust treatment of Ireland by the English government. One of the most famous is ____.

A. *Essays on Criticism*
B. *A Modest Proposal*
C. *Gulliver's Travels*
D. *The Battle of the Books*

101. ____ the first important work by Tobias Smollett, is based on his own experience as a naval doctor and in part autobiographical.

A. *Roderick Random*
B. *Humphry Clinker*
C. *Peregrine Pickle*
D. *A Sentimental Journey*

102. The 18th century witnessed that in England there appeared two political parties, ______, which were satirized by Jonathan Swift in his *Gulliver's Travels*.

A. The Whigs and the Tories
B. The Senate and the House of Representatives
C. The Upper House and Lower House
D. The House of Lords and the House of Commons

103. _____compiled the *A Dictionary ofthe English Language* which became the foundation of all the subsequent English dictionaries.

A. Ben Johnson
B. Samuel Johnson
C. Alexander Pope
D. John Dryden

104. The main literary stream is ____ in English Romantic Age.

A. poetry
B. novels

C. prose D. periodicals

105. ____ has a another name called "The Daffodils".

A. "The Rime of the Ancient Mariner" B. "Tintern Abbey"

C. "Revolution" D. "I Wandered Lonely as a Cloud"

106. *Prometheus Unbound* is ____ masterpiece.

A. Wordsworth's B. Byron's

C. Shelley's D. Keats'

107. The publication of ______ marks the beginning of the Romantic Movement in England.

A. "Tintern Abbey" B. *Lyrical Ballads*

C. *Frost at Night* D. "The Daffodils"

108. *The Prelude* has also been called _____.

A. *The Last Brazil* B. *The First Impression*

C. *Growth of a Poet's Mind* D. *The Spirit of the Age*

109. Wordsworth's "I Wandered Lonely as a Cloud" has also been called _______.

A. "The Solitary Reaper" B. "The Daffodils"

C. "The Rime of the Ancient Mariner" D. "O Solitude"

110. The best essayist in the English Romantic Age is _____.

A. Keats B. Walter Scott

C. Charles Lamb D. William Hazlitt

111. The themes of *Pride and Prejudice* are _____.

A. pride and prejudice B. the writer's own personalities

C. love and marriage D. Both A and C

112. Because of _______, Shelley was expelled from the Oxford University.

A. *The Masque of Anarchy* B. *A Defence of Poetry*

C. *The Necessity of Atheism* D. *The Triumph of Life*

113. The Romantic Age began in____ and came to an end in _____.

A. 1789…1821 B. 1778…1823

C. 1798…1832 D. 1768…1819

114. ______'s *Vanity Fair* is a satirical portrayal of the upper strata(阶层) of society.

A. George Eliot B. Elizabeth Gaskell

C. W. M. Thackeray D. John Buyan

115. Emily Bronte wrote only one novel entitled ______.

A. *Jane Eyre* B. *Agnes Grey*

C. *Wuthering Heights* D. *Emma*

116. The Victorian Literature began in____ and ended in _____.

A. 1837…1901 B. 1835…1901

C. 1832…1902 D. 1830…1903

117. _____ is the greatest among the critical realists of the Victorian Age.

A. Earnest Jones B. Emily Brontë

C. Charlotte Brontë D. Charles Dickens

118. The two cities in *A Tale of Two Cities* refer to ____.

A. London and New York B. London and Paris

C. Paris and New York D. Brussels and Washington

119. ____ is the major literary form in the Victorian Period.

A. Essay B. Poetry

C. Novel D. Drama

120. The most important poet in the Victorian Age was _____.

A. Earnest Jones B. Elizabeth Gaskell

C. Mr. Browning D. Alfred Tennyson

121. Tennyson's _____ expresses his optimistic attitude towards death when he is old.

A. *Break, Break, Break* B. *Crossing the Bar*

C. *The Princess* D. *Maud*

122. Henry James is the forerunner of the _____.

A. Imagism B. Chartism

C. impressionism D. stream of consciousness

123. Katharine Mansfield is a master of ____ at the turn of the century.

A. short story writer B. dramatic poetry

C. realistic novels D. humor

124. John Galsworthy won the Nobel Prize for Literature because of _____.

A. *The End of the Chapter* B. *The Forsyte Saga*

C. *A Modern Comedy* D. *The Island Pharisees*

Part 3 Analysis

1. D. 小说《爱玛》的作者是 Jane Austen。
2. B. George Elliot 不是浪漫派诗人，她是小说家。
3. A. Elliot 是 20 世纪诗人。
4. D. Emily Bronte 是 *Wuthering Heights* 的作者。
5. C. Yeats 是爱尔兰诗人和剧作家。
6. B. *The Canterbury Tales* 的作者是 Geoffrey Chaucer。
7. A. 除 George Eliot 外，其他几位都是 20 世纪英国著名女作家。
8. D. *Ode to the West Wind* 的作者是 Percy Bysshe Shelley。
9. C. *Sons and Lovers* 的作者是 D. H. Lawrence。
10. C. Robert Browning 擅长戏剧独白，是维多利亚时期代表诗人之一。
11. A. 可以通过排除法排除 B、C、D，进而选择 A. 寓言。
12. D. Virginia Woolf 是英国著名小说家。
13. C. epic 是“史诗、叙事诗”的意思。
14. A. *Beowulf* 是英国盎格鲁－撒克逊时期的一首英雄史诗。
15. D. Virginia Woolf 和 James Joyce 是英国意识流小说家的重要代表。
16. A.《尤利西斯》*Ulysses*、《都柏林人》*Dubliners*、《一个青年艺术家的画像》*A Portrait of the Artist as a Young Man* 及《芬尼根守灵夜》*Finnegans Wake* 是 James Joyce 的作品。
17. A. George Orwell 是 20 世纪著名的社会批评家。他的代表作：*Animal Farm* 和 *1984*。
18. A. *Jane Eyre* 与 *Wuthering Heights* 的作者分别为 Charlotte Bronte 和 Emily Bronte，两人为姐妹。其他选项错误。
19. C. 哥尔德斯密斯（*Oliver Goldsmith*，1730—1774），英国剧作家、小说家。不是维多利亚时期的诗人。
20. B. 小说是维多利亚文学的主流形式。
21. A. 奥斯卡·王尔德与乔治·萧伯纳是维多利亚时期的两位杰出剧作家。
22. A. 约翰·邓恩（John Donne）是 17 世纪玄学派诗人。
23. A.《荒原》（*The Waste Land*）（1922）是 20 世纪西方文学里一部划时代的作品，是现代派诗歌的里程碑，也是艾略特的成名作。

24. A. 华兹华斯（William Wordsworth，1770—1850），英国浪漫主义诗人，曾当上桂冠诗人。其诗歌理论动摇了英国古典主义诗学的统治，有力地推动了英国诗歌的革新和浪漫主义运动的发展。华兹华斯认为“所有的好诗都是强烈情感的自然流露”（the spontaneous overflow of powerful emotion），是其对诗歌的一个重要定义。
25. C. 罗伯特·彭斯（Robert Burns，1759 年 1 月 25 日—1796 年 7 月 21 日），苏格兰农民诗人，在英国文学史上占有特殊重要的地位。他复活并丰富了苏格兰民歌，他的诗歌富有音乐性，可以歌唱。
26. A. 塞缪尔·约翰逊（Samuel Johnson）是英国作家、文学评论家和诗人，经九年奋斗，终于编成《英语大辞典》（1755），即《约翰逊字典》。
27. A. *Lord of the Flies*，中文译作《蝇王》，是英国作家、诺贝尔文学奖获得者威廉·戈尔丁的代表作，是一本重要的哲理小说，借小孩的天真来探讨“人性的恶”这一严肃主题。
28. A. 玛丽·安·伊文思（Mary Ann Evans，1819—1880），笔名乔治·艾略特，英国小说家、诗人、记者、翻译家，维多利亚时代的著名作家之一。她的小说清新优美，极富田园生活中大自然的气息，流露出她对田园生活的喜爱和向往，其代表作有《罗莫拉》《米德尔马契》和《弗洛斯河上的磨坊》。
29. D. 托马斯·哈代不是现代主义作家。
30. D. 小说《恋爱中的女人》（*Woman in love*）由英国作家 D. H. Lawrence 所著，并于 1920 年出版。
31. A. 杰弗雷·乔叟（Geoffrey Chaucer）首创的英雄双韵体为以后的英国诗人所广泛采用，被誉为“英国诗歌之父”。
32. D.《海浪》（*The Waves*）是英国女作家弗吉尼亚·伍尔芙 1931 年创作的长篇小说，作者以极具朦胧意味和象征意味的笔触描绘了六个人物：伯纳德、内维尔、路易斯、苏珊、珍妮和罗达从童稚到垂暮之年的内心独白，用六股平行的意识流分别表现了意识的六种类型和“人的六个时代”的成长经历和体验。
33. A.《失乐园》（*Paradise Lost*）是英国政治家、学者约翰·弥尔顿创作的史诗。
34. C.《哈姆雷特》（*Hamlet*）是莎士比亚最负盛名的一部悲剧。

35. C. 弗兰西斯·培根（1561—1626），英国哲学家、文学家、法学家、政治家，著有《学术之进步》《新工具》《新大西岛》和《随笔集》等。《培根随笔集》共 58 篇，内容涉及人类生活的方方面面。包括“论真理”“论死亡”“论人的天性”“论高官”“论王权”“论野心”“论爱情”“论友情”“论婚姻与独身”等。语言简洁，文笔优美，说理透彻，警句迭出，几百年来深受各国读者喜爱。

36. B.“To be, or not to be, that is a question.”为《哈姆雷特》中的一句独白。

37. A. 文艺复兴是一场哲学和文学运动，同时文艺复兴强调教育，其对政治体制的演变没有特殊的影响。

38. C. 诗集《坎特伯雷故事集》为杰弗雷·乔叟的主要作品。

39. C. 乌托邦（Utopia）本意为“没有的地方”或者“好地方”。延伸为还有理想，不可能完成的好事情，其中文翻译也可以理解为“乌”是没有，“托”是寄托，“邦”是国家，“乌托邦”三个字合起来的意思即“空想的国家”。空想社会主义的创始人托马斯·莫尔（英国人）在他的名著《乌托邦》中虚构了一个航海家航行到一个奇乡异国“乌托邦”的旅行见闻。

40. C. 约翰·弥尔顿（John Milton，1608 年 12 月 9 日—1674 年 11 月 8 日）英国诗人、政论家、民主斗士。代表作品有长诗《失乐园》《复乐园》和《力士参孙》。

41. D.《李尔王》是莎士比亚四大悲剧之一，故事讲述了年事已高的国王李尔王退位后，被大女儿和二女儿赶到荒郊野外。成为法兰西皇后的三女儿率军救父，却被杀死，李尔王伤心地死在她身旁。雪莱称《李尔王》是世界上最完美的戏剧诗的样本。

42. D.《鲁滨逊漂流记》（*Robinson Crusoe*）是丹尼尔·笛福创作的长篇小说。

43. A. 亚历山大·蒲柏（Alexander Pope），1688 年 5 月 22 日 出生于伦敦，是 18 世纪英国最伟大的诗人，杰出的启蒙主义者。他推动了英国新古典主义文学的发展。

44. A. 解析同 43 题。

45. C. 小说《项狄传》（*The Life and Opinions of Tristram Shandy*）是劳伦斯·斯特恩的代表作品。

46. C. 18 世纪英国小说兴起。这一时期最有成就的作家是 Daniel Defoe、Jonathan Swift、Henry Fielidng 等。

47. A. 18 世纪五六十年代感伤主义盛行于英国，感伤主义的名称源自斯泰恩的小说《感伤的旅行》，而感伤主义更常见于诗歌。
48. A.《四个四重奏》（*Four Quartets*）作者是托马斯·斯特尔那斯·艾略特（T. S. Eliot）。
49. C. 威廉·布莱克（William Blake），英国第一位重要的浪漫主义诗人、英国文学史上最重要的伟大诗人之一，主要诗作有诗集《纯真之歌》（*Songs of Innocence*）、《经验之歌》*Songs of Experience* 等。
50. C.《往昔的时光》（*Auld Lang Syne*）为苏格兰诗人罗伯特·彭斯（Robert Burns）代表作品之一。
51. D. 英国积极浪漫主义诗人主要有拜伦（Byron）、雪莱（Shelley）和济慈（Keats）。沃尔特·司各特（Walter Scott）是英国著名的历史小说家和诗人。
52. D.《忽必烈汗》（*Kubla Khan*）为英国诗人柯勒律治的作品。
53. B. 英国消极浪漫主义诗人主要有华兹华斯、柯勒律治、骚塞。B《古舟子咏》（*The Rime of the Ancient Mariner*）为柯勒律治的作品。
54. A. 威廉·哈兹里特（Hazlitt William），英国散文家，评论家，画家。其文艺批评作品《莎士比亚戏剧中的人物》以优美流畅的散文笔调书写自己阅读和观看莎士比亚戏剧的独特感受，既有对情节、人物、台词等方面深刻细致的分析，又有对舞台演出精彩独到的点评。莎士比亚的戏剧天才通过哈兹里特的评论以一种特别的面貌完美地展现在人们面前，此书在浩如烟海的莎士比亚研究著作中占有重要地位，是了解莎剧的优秀作品。
55. D. 查尔斯·兰姆（1775—1834），英国散文家，其主要作品有《莎士比亚故事集》（*Tales from Shakespeare*）、《伊利亚散文集》（*Essays of Llia*），《英国戏剧诗人的标本》（*Specimens of English Dramatic Poets*）等。D.《莎士比亚戏剧集序言》（*The Preface to Shakespeare*），是塞缪尔·约翰逊（Samuel Johnson）的作品。
56. A. 浪漫主义诗人拜伦（Lord Byron）撰写了唐璜故事的叙事诗版本——唐·璜（Don Juan），被公认为他的经典之作。
57. C.《致云雀》（*To a Skylark*）是英国诗人珀西·比希·雪莱创作于 1820 年的诗歌。
58. C.《乡村墓园挽歌》（*Elegy Written in a Country Churchyard*）是托马斯·格雷（Thomas Gray）的代表作，他把伤感文学推向了顶峰。

59. A.《荒原》(*The Waste Land*) 作者是托马斯·斯特尔那斯·艾略特 (T. S. Eliot)。
60. A. 托马斯·艾略特 (T. S. Eliot) 是英国现代主义诗歌运动的领袖，是诗歌创作技巧的伟大改良者。
61. A. 18 世纪英国小说兴起。这一时期最有成就的作家是丹尼尔·笛福 (Daniel Defoe)、乔纳森·斯威夫特 (Jonathan Swift)、亨利·菲尔丁 (Henry Fielding) 等。简·奥斯汀 (Jane Austin)、查尔斯·狄更斯 (Charles Dickens)、乔治·艾略特 (George Eliot) 都是19世纪英国小说家。
62. C. 奥利弗·哥德史密斯 (Oliver Goldsmith) 是 18 世纪著名的英国剧作家。
63. A. Oliver Twist 为《雾都孤儿》小说作品中的人物名。
64. D.《弗洛斯河上的磨坊》(*The Mill on the Floss*) 是英国作家乔治·艾略特创作的长篇小说。
65. B.《名利场》(*Vanity Fair*) 是 19 世纪英国批判现实主义作家威廉·梅克比斯·萨克雷创作的长篇小说。
66. A. 约瑟夫·康拉德 (Joseph Conrad)，英国作家，擅长写海洋冒险小说，《黑暗的心》是其最负盛誉的小说。
67. A. 爱德华·摩根·福斯特 (E. M. Forster)，20 世纪英国作家。其主要作品有小说《看得见风景的房间》《霍华德庄园》《印度之行》等。
68. A.《德伯家的苔丝》是英国作家哈代的长篇小说，是“威塞克斯系列”中的一部。
69. B.《艾凡赫》(*Ivanhoe*) 是英国作家沃尔特·司各特创作的长篇历史小说。
70. C.《圣女贞德》是爱尔兰剧作家乔治·伯纳德·萧伯纳 (George Bernard Shaw) 的代表作品之一。
71. A. 赫伯特·乔治·威尔斯 (Herbert George Wells) 是英国著名小说家、新闻记者、政治家、社会学家和历史学家。代表作品有《时间机器》《莫洛博士岛》《隐身人》《星际战争》等。
72. B. 简·奥斯汀 (Jane Austen)，英国女小说家，主要作品有《傲慢与偏见》《理智与情感》《曼斯菲尔德庄园》《爱玛》和《劝导》等。A、C、D 作品为勃朗特姐妹的作品。
73. D. 托马斯·哈代，英国诗人、小说家。哈代是横跨两个世纪的作家，早期和中期的创作以小说为主，继承和发扬了维多利亚时代的文学传统；晚年其诗歌推动了英国 20 世纪的文学发展。

74. A. 詹姆斯 · 乔伊斯的《尤利西斯》被广泛认为是一部文学杰作，也是最难读的文学作品之一。
75. B. 詹姆斯 · 乔伊斯是“意识流”写作技巧的大师。
76. D. 小说《恋爱中的女人》（*Women in Love*）由英国作家 D. H. Lawrence 所著，并于 1920 年出版。
77. B.《爱玛》（*Emma*）为英国小说家简 · 奥斯汀（Jane Austen）的作品。
78. A.《荒原》（*The Waste Land*）（1922）是艾略特的成名作，是 20 世纪西方文学一部划时代的作品，是现代派诗歌的里程碑。
79. A.《驶向拜占庭》（*Sailing to Byzantium*）是爱尔兰诗人叶芝的代表作之一。
80. D. 意识流文学泛指注重描绘人物意识流动状态的文学作品，既包括清醒的意识，也包括无意识、梦幻意识和语言前意识。意识流文学是现代主义文学的重要分支，主要成就局限在小说领域，在戏剧、诗歌中也有表现。詹姆斯 · 乔伊斯、维吉尼亚 · 伍尔芙、亨利 · 詹姆斯都是意识流的代表作家。
81. A.《动物庄园》（*Animal Farm*）亦译作《动物农场》《动物农庄》，是乔治 · 奥威尔创作的中篇小说，1945 年首次出版。
82. C. 多丽丝 · 莱辛（Doris Lessing），笔名简 · 萨默斯，2007 年凭借代表作《金色笔记》获得诺贝尔文学奖提名以及多个世界级文学奖项。她以怀疑主义、激情和想象力审视一个被拉开的文明，登上了这方面女性体验的史诗巅峰。
83. B. 高尔斯华绥代表作品有《福尔赛世家》三部曲（《有产业的人》《骑虎》《出租》）和《现代喜剧》三部曲（《白猿》《银匙》《天鹅曲》）等。因此选择 B 选项。
84. D.《河湾》（*A Bend in the River*）是奈保尔（V. S. Naipaul）代表作之一。
85. A.《法国中尉的女人》（*The French Lieutenant's Woman*）由约翰 · 福尔斯所著，是英国实验主义文学的杰作。
86. B. 简 · 奥斯汀（1775—1817）是英国第一位重要的女性小说家。
87. A.《儿子与情人》（*Sons and Lovers*）是劳伦斯最重要的小说之一，这部小说是作者的半自传体小说。
88. D. 乔治 · 奥威尔。1923 年，叶芝获得诺贝尔文学奖；1983 年，威廉 · 戈尔丁获诺贝尔文学奖；2007 年，多丽丝·莱辛荣获诺贝尔文学奖。

89. A.《荒原》是现代主义诗歌的代表作。

90. A. 乔叟（Geoffrey Chaucer）是英国诗歌的奠基人，被后人誉为“英国诗歌之父”。

91. D. 乔叟于 1400 年在伦敦去世，葬于威斯敏斯特教堂的“诗人之角”。

92. D. 托马斯·莫尔的《乌托邦》是世界文学史上第一部具有广泛影响的宣传空想社会主义思想的杰作，分为上、下两部。用作者和航海家两人对话的形式写成。

93. A. 莎士比亚戏剧的语言形式既以无韵诗为主，又杂有古体诗、民谣体、俚谚与轻快滑稽的散文体对话，可谓多种多样、丰富生动。

94. C. 莎士比亚文学是英国文艺复兴时期文学领域的发展顶峰。

95. A. 理查德·斯梯尔（Richard Steele）是与约瑟夫·艾迪生齐名的散文家。1708 年，他创办了著名的《闲话报》（*The Tatler*），后来又与艾迪生合办杂志《旁观者》（*The Spectator*）。

96. A. 解析同上题。

97. B. 亚历山大·蒲柏（Alexander Pope），是 18 世纪英国最伟大的诗人，杰出的启蒙主义者。他推动英国新古典主义文学发展，代表作有《夺发记》（*The Rape of the Lock*）、《愚人志》（*The Dunciad*）等。

98. B. 现实主义作家在他们的作品中进行社会现实的描述。

99. D. 18 世纪是小说的黄金时代。

100. B. 斯威夫特通过《一个小小的建议》（*A Modest Proposal*），深刻揭露了爱尔兰的社会矛盾，控诉了英格兰统治者和爱尔兰地主的残酷剥削，而对广大的爱尔兰穷苦人民表露出深深的同情。文章的通篇内容都是以一种辛辣的讽刺和机敏的反语表达的。

101. A. 托比亚斯·乔治·斯摩莱特（Tobias Smollett）作为 18 世纪最伟大的小说家之一，擅长撰写讽刺喜剧，以讽刺手法刻画社会各个阶层中的人物。处女作《蓝登传》（1748 年）在很大程度上是一部自传性作品，讲述了一位苏格兰年轻人力图发财致富的故事，其中包括许多发生在海军船只上的鲜活场景。

102. A.《格列佛游记》是英国作家乔纳森·斯威夫特创作的一部长篇游记体讽刺小说。作品以里梅尔·格列佛（又译为莱缪尔·格列佛）船长的口气叙述周游四国的经历。通过格列佛在利立浦特、布罗卜丁奈格、飞岛国、慧骃国的奇遇，反映了 18 世纪前半期英国统治阶级的腐败和罪恶。小说第一卷所描绘的小人国的情景是当时大英帝国的缩影。对当时托利党和辉格党常年不息的斗争和对外的战争，实质上只是政客们在一些国计民生毫不相干的小节上钩心斗角进行了讽刺与批判。

103. B. 塞缪尔·约翰逊（Samuel Johnson）是英国作家、文学评论家和诗人，经九年奋斗，终于编成《英语大辞典》(1755)，即《约翰逊字典》(*A Dictionary of the English Language*）。

104. A. 英国浪漫主义文学时期小说、诗歌、戏剧等文学形式都有，主要以诗歌为代表。

105. D. 华兹华斯（William Wordsworth，1770—1850 年)，英国浪漫主义诗人，曾当上桂冠诗人。代表诗作《水仙花》(*The Daffodils*)，又译作《我好似一朵流云独自漫游》。

106. C.《解放了的普罗米修斯》(*Prometheus Unbound*）是英国浪漫主义诗人雪莱创作的诗剧，取材于古希腊罗马神话和埃斯库罗斯的悲剧，发表于 1819 年。

107. B.《抒情歌谣集》(*Lyrical Ballads*）宣告了浪漫主义新诗的诞生。华兹华斯在 1800 年《抒情歌谣集》第二版的序言中详细阐述了浪漫主义新诗的理论，主张以平民的语言抒写平民的事物、思想与感情，被誉为浪漫主义诗歌的宣言。

108. C. 华兹华斯写了一整本诗体自传，题名《序曲——一个诗人心灵的成长》，开创了自传诗的新形式。

109. B. 华兹华斯（William Wordsworth)，代表诗作《我好似一朵流云独自漫游》(*I Wandered Lonely as a Cloud*)，又译作《水仙花》(*The Daffodils*)。

110. C. 英国浪漫时代最具代表性的散文家是查尔斯·兰姆。

111. D.《傲慢与偏见》主题的体现为 A 与 C。

112. C. 珀西·比希·雪莱（Percy Bysshe Shelley）因刊行《论无神论的必然性》一文而被牛津大学开除。

113. C. 英国浪漫主义时期一般被认为始于 1798 年，标志为华兹华斯与柯勒律治的《抒情歌谣集》的出版，终于 1832 年，标志为沃尔特·司各特的去世及英国议会第一次改革法案的通过。

114. C. 威廉·梅克比斯·萨克雷（William Makepeace Thackeray），与狄更斯齐名，为维多利亚时代的代表小说家。其代表作品是世界名著《名利场》。

115. C. 艾米莉·勃朗特（Emily Bronte），19 世纪英国作家与诗人，著名的勃朗特三姐妹之一，世界文学名著《呼啸山庄》的作者。这部作品是艾米莉·勃朗特一生中唯一的一部小说，奠定了她在英国文学史以及世界文学史上的地位。此外，她还创作了 193 首诗，被认为是英国一位天才型的女作家。

116. A. 维多利亚文学时限常被定义为 1837—1901 年，即维多利亚女王（Alexandrina Victoria）的统治时期。

117. D. 狄更斯生活和创作的时间，正是 19 世纪中叶维多利亚女王时代前期。狄更斯毕生的活动和创作，始终与时代潮流同步。他以写实笔法揭露社会上层和资产阶级的虚伪、贪婪、卑琐、凶残，满怀激愤和深切的同情展示下层社会，特别是妇女、儿童和老人的悲惨处境，并以严肃、慎重的态度描写开始觉醒的劳苦大众的抗争。与此同时，他还以理想主义和浪漫主义的豪情讴歌人性中的真、善、美，憧憬更合理的社会和更美好的人生。狄更斯是维多利亚时代最伟大的批判现实主义作家。

118. B.《双城记》（*A Tale of Two Cities*）是英国作家查尔斯·狄更斯所著的一部长篇历史小说，双城是指巴黎和伦敦两大城市。

119. C. 小说是维多利亚时期的主要文学形式。

120. D. 阿尔弗雷德·丁尼生（Alfredlord Tennyson），是英国维多利亚时代最受欢迎及最具特色的诗人。代表作品为组诗《悼念》。

121. A. Break, Break, Break 表达了丁尼生对死亡的乐观态度。

122. D. 亨利·詹姆斯（HenryJames）是小说家、文学批评家、剧作家和散文家，被一致认为是心理分析小说的开创者之一，他对人的行为的认识有独到之处，是 20 世纪小说的意识流写作技巧的先驱。

123. A. 凯瑟琳·曼斯菲尔德（Katherine Mansfield，1888—1923），是世纪之交的短篇小说家。

124. B. 1932 年，高尔斯华绥的《福尔赛世家》因“为其描述的卓越艺术——这种艺术在《福尔赛世家》中达到高峰”（“or his distinguished art of narration which takes its highest form in The Forsyte Saga”）而荣获诺贝尔文学奖。